The Sci-Fi Factor

Perfection Learning®

Editorial Director Julie A. Schumacher, Carol Francis

Senior Editor Terry Ofner

Permissions Lisa Lorimor

Reviewer Charles Shields

Design and Photo Research William Seabright and Associates, Wilmette, Illinois

Cover Art HOT SUMMER NIGHT Gayle Denington-Anderson

Acknowledgments

"A.D. 2267" by John Frederick Nims. Originally printed in *Of Flesh and Bone* by John Frederick Nims. Published by Rutgers University Press. Printed by permission of Bonnie Nims.

"All Watched Over by Machines of Loving Grace" from *The Pill Versus the Springhill Mine Disaster*. Copyright © 1965 by Richard Brautigan. Reprinted by permission of Houghton Mifflin Company. All rights reserved.

"Backward Step" by Paul Jennings from *Uncovered*! Reprinted by permission of Penguin Books Australia Ltd.

"Dark They Were, and Golden-Eyed" by Ray Bradbury. Reprinted by permission of Don Congdon Associates, Inc. Copyright © 1949 by Standard Magazines, renewed 1976 by Ray Bradbury.

"The Helping Hand" by Norman Spinrad. Copyright © 1991 by Norman Spinrad. Reprinted by permission of the author.

"In Communication with a UFO" by Helen Chasin. Copyright © 1998 by Yale University. Published in The Yale Younger Poets Anthology.

"Lose Now, Pay Later" by Carol Farley. Reprinted by permission of GRM Associates, Inc., from the book *2041: Twelve Stories About the Future*, copyright © 1968.

"Mariana" by Fritz Leiber. Published in *Fantastic*. Reprinted by permission of The Richard Curtis Agency.

"A Martian Sends a Postcard Home" by Craig Raine. Reprinted by permission of David Godwin Associates.

"Minister Without Portfolio" by Mildred Clingerman. Reprin-ted by permission of Stuart Clingerman. Originally published in *Fantasy & Science Fiction*, February 1952.

CONTINUED ON PAGE 160

10 11 12 13 14 PP 18 17 16 15 14 13

78865
PB ISBN: 978-0-7891-2848-5
RLB ISBN: 978-0-7807-9701-7

Printed in the United States of America

What's the Fascination with Science Fiction?

The question above is the *essential question* that you will consider as you read this book. The literature, activities, and organization of the book will lead you to think critically about this question, to understand the elements of science fiction writing, and, perhaps, to become one of the millions of avid science fiction readers around the world.

To help you shape your answer to the broad essential question, you will read and respond to four sections, or clusters, of literature. Each cluster addresses a specific question and thinking skill.

CLUSTER ONE What's the 'science' in science fiction? **ANALYZING**

CLUSTER TWO Who's out there? **HYPOTHESIZING**

CLUSTER THREE What can we learn from science fiction? **DRAWING CONCLUSIONS**

CLUSTER FOUR Thinking on your own **SYNTHESIZING**

Notice that the final cluster asks you to think independently about your answer to the essential question—*What's the fascination with science fiction?*

Square in the eye!! from the 1902 film *A Trip to the Moon*
Georges Méliès

A.D. 2267

Once on the gritty moon (burnt earth hung far

In the black, rhinestone sky—lopsided star),

Two gadgets, with great fishbowls for a head,

Feet clubbed, hips loaded, shoulders bent. She said,

"Fantasies haunt me. A green garden. Two

Lovers aglow in flesh. The pools so blue!"

He whirrs with masculine pity, "Can't forget

Old superstitions? The earth-legend yet?"

John Frederick Nims

The Sci-Fi Factor

Crescent Earth over the Lunar Highlands,
Apollo 15
1971

Table of Contents

"Beam me up, Scotty"

science n. knowledge based on observed facts and tested truths arranged in an orderly system.

fiction n. 1 novels, short stories, and other prose writings that tell about imaginary people and happenings. 2 something imagined or made up.

Science and fiction, it seems, are polar opposites. Science deals with proven or provable facts; fiction deals with imagination and fancy. Science drives new advances, from medicine to transportation to communication; fiction creates imaginary worlds populated with people who never existed. Science is carried out by experimenters wearing white coats in laboratories; fiction is practiced by artists struggling with words in solitude. Despite the differences, or perhaps because of them, the marriage of science and fiction produces one of the most lively genres, or forms of literature—science fiction, or sci-fi for short.

Consider the command, "Beam me up, Scotty" from the sci-fi television series *Star Trek*. The idea is simple: as a transporter beam disassembles the traveler, it extracts all the information needed to describe the individual. The information is beamed across space to a receiving station where the person is reassembled. Science fiction at its best. Or is it? Recently, researchers in quantum physics have successfully teleported the quantum state of an atom across space. Could Scotty's transporter room be far behind?

Whatever the results of research in quantum transport technology, it appears that the distance between science and fiction is narrowing. As sci-fi writers dream, scientists are busy bringing those dreams into reality. And as scientists bring forth new technologies and discoveries, sci-fi writers are busy asking questions, warning of potential dangers, pushing at the boundaries of the known. For if there is one thing that both scientists and science fiction writers share, it is their love of frontiers. Both travel along the boundary between the known and the unknown. Both seek to expand understanding of our universe and ourselves.

As you explore the following pages, let the literature of sci-fi beam you up into that uncharted territory where the dreams of today and the science of tomorrow converge.

Concept Vocabulary

You will find the following terms and definitions useful as you read and discuss the selections in this book.

alien a nonhuman being from somewhere other than Earth

android a human-like robot

asteroid any of the small celestial bodies found between the orbits of Mars and Jupiter

black hole a region of space with a gravitation field so strong that not even light can escape from it

close encounter contact between a human and a UFO or occupant of a UFO as defined by those investigating UFO phenomena. *Close Encounter of the First Kind:* observation of a UFO from a distance; *of the Second Kind:* observation of physical evidence left behind by a UFO; *of the Third Kind:* observation of an entity or occupant of a UFO; *of the Fourth Kind:* abduction of a human by an occupant of a UFO

cosmos the universe

dystopia a utopia where conditions become intolerable. *See also* utopia.

extraterrestrial anything not on or from Earth. *See also* alien.

galaxy (galactic) any very large cluster of stars and other matter such as the Milky Way

hyperspace a fictional kind of space in which extraordinary events such as traveling faster than the speed of light can occur

interstellar among the stars

nova a star that suddenly increases its light output

robot (robotics) a machine capable of performing human tasks

sentient being aware of sensory perceptions such as touch, taste, etc.

speed of light 186,000 miles per second, a speed impossible to exceed according to Einstein's theories of relativity

terraforming making another planet habitable for human life

time paradox an impossible situation created by traveling back through time, for example, when a man travels back and kills his father, so that he himself could never have existed

time travel moving backward or forward in time

time warp a distortion in the normal flow of time

utopia a fictional ideal society. *See also* dystopia

UFO an unidentified flying object

CLUSTER ONE

What's the 'Science' in Science Fiction?

Thinking Skill ANALYZING

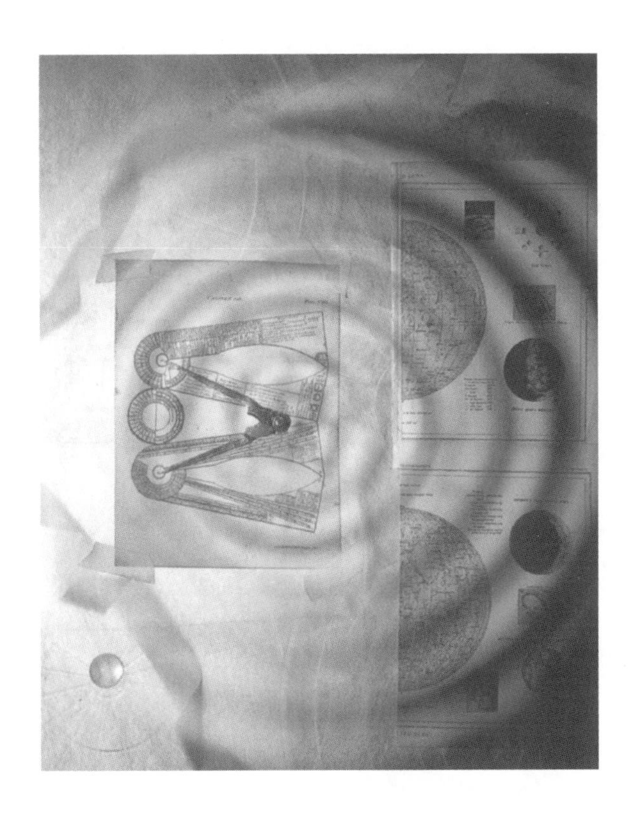

Backward Step

PAUL JENNINGS

If you went back in time and stopped your grandparents from meeting each other, you would never have been born. But then if you had never been born, you wouldn't be able to go back to stop them. Would you?

"John," said Mrs. Booth to her five-year-old son. "You just sit there and watch 'Inspector Gadget' on the TV while I go down the street and get some milk. I'll be back by the time it's over."

"I love 'Inspector Gadget,'" said John.

Mrs. Booth reached the front gate and then stopped. She felt a little guilty, leaving her son alone in the house. But she knew he wouldn't budge. Not for another twenty minutes. Not until the show was over.

"Excuse me, Mrs. Booth," said a voice.

She jumped in fright and then stared into the eyes of a teenage boy. He thrust an old exercise book into her hand. "Read this. Please, please, please read it."

"I'm not interested in buying . . ." she began to say.

"I'm not selling anything," he said. "And it's not a religion. This is important. This can save your life. You're in great danger. Please read it."

"Now?" she said.

"Right away. Please, it's really important."

There was something about the boy. He seemed very nervous. And she felt as if she knew him. The boy's hands were shaking. "Well," she said. "Just for a second." She gave a little sigh and opened the old exercise book.

I am fourteen. Nine years ago I was also fourteen. And nine years before that I was fourteen, too.

It is creepy. It is weird. But I think I have figured it all out. It makes sense to me now. It is the only explanation. No one will believe me, of course. They will just say I am crazy.

Look—I'll try and explain it to you as simply as I can. I've put one and one together and come up with two. Or should I say I've put nine and five together and come up with five.

No, no, no, that's just talking in riddles. I'll start at the beginning. Or is it the end?

Sorry, there I go again. Look, have you ever wanted strange powers? You know, to be able to fly or read thoughts or be very strong? I'll bet you think it would be great. But think again. It could be dangerous. You could end up hurting yourself. Like I did.

I am famous. Yes, there wouldn't be too many people around here who haven't heard of me. I'll bet you think it would be great to be famous. Pictures in the paper. On television. People wanting your autograph. That sort of thing.

It's not really that good. You never know whether people want to be your friend because they like you or because you are well known. And then there are kids who get jealous and give you a hard time and push you around. I would rather be ordinary and have ordinary problems.

I became famous at five. They called me the boy from nowhere. There was a great fuss. It was in the papers. A five-year-old boy just suddenly appeared, sitting in the back seat of the class. Right next to a girl called Sharon Coppersmith.

That boy was me.

Sharon Coppersmith screamed and screamed when I arrived. Or appeared. According to her I just popped out of nowhere. One minute the seat was empty. The next minute there was little old me. Five years old, sitting next to her in a history class.

All the big kids crowded around. They were glad to have something to break up the lesson. They laughed and offered me candy and made a great fuss. The teacher thought that I had wandered in from the street.

I just looked up and started crying. I was only five but I remember it just like it was yesterday. Who were all these big kids? Where was my mummy? Where was the nice big boy who wanted to help me?

"What's your name, little fellah?" said the teacher.

For a while I couldn't get a word out. I just sat there sobbing. In the end I managed to say, "John Boof, firteen Tower Street, Upwey, seven five four, oh, oh, six two free free."

"'John Booth,'" said the teacher. " 'Thirteen Tower Street, Upwey. Phone 754, 0, 0, 6233.' Well done. Don't cry, little fellah. We'll have you home in no time."

2

The principal's office seemed huge. He wore a pair of those little half-moon glasses and kept peeping over them at me while he spoke into the phone. "Are you sure?" he said. "754, 0, 0, 6233. No John Booth? Never heard of him. How long have you lived there? Three years. Well, sorry to have troubled you."

I just kept licking the salty tears that were rolling down my cheek and wondering how I got there.

I had been watching "Inspector Gadget" on television. I remember the man saying something like, "A brand-new episode." Then a big boy was talking to me. He just popped out of nowhere. He was nice. I was holding his hand and then *poof*, he was gone and there I was sitting in this schoolroom full of big kids. With everyone looking at me and wondering where I had come from.

"Look," said the principal to his secretary. "Pop him in your car and see if he can show you where he lives. If he can't find the place, you'll have to take him to the police station. His parents will come for him sooner or later."

I knew that I didn't have a father. But I didn't know that my mother had died nine years earlier.

The secretary was nice. She strapped me into the seat next to her and gave me a little white bag with jelly beans in it. "Don't worry, love," she said. "We'll soon find Mum. You just show me the way to go. All you have to do is point."

She drove around for a bit and I thought I recognized some of the houses and places. But they were different. Looking back I can describe it as like being in a dream. The streets were the same but different.

"There," I suddenly yelled. It was the water tower. I could see it in the distance. It was right next to our house.

"What?" said the nice lady. "The water tower? You couldn't live there, love."

"Neks door," I said.

She smiled. "Now we're getting somewhere."

There was only one house next to the water tower and it was my house. At least it was like my house. It had the same rock chimney and the same fountain in the front yard. But it was painted green instead of blue. And the trees were huge. And the chicken shed had gone. But it was still my house.

"Mummy," I shouted. I had never been so happy in my life. I didn't stop to think that you can't paint a house in one day. And that trees can't grow overnight. When you are five you think adults can do anything. I raced up to the front door and ran inside. Then I just stopped and stared. Our furniture had gone. There was no television. My photo wasn't on the wall.

"Mummy," I screamed. "Mummy, Mummy, Mummy." I scampered into the kitchen. A very old lady looked down at me. Then she looked at the secretary who had followed me in and started to scream.

The old lady thought we had come to rob her.

After all, we had just walked into her house without even knocking.

3

Well, after a lot of talking, the secretary managed to calm the old lady down. They had a cup of tea and the old lady gave me some green cordial.[1] "Mummy," I said. "I want my mummy." I didn't know what this old lady was doing in our house. I didn't know where my toys had gone. I didn't like the new carpet and the photos of strange people. I wanted everything to be like it was before. I also wanted to go to the toilet.

I ran upstairs, through the big bedroom and into the little toilet at the back. When I came back I heard the secretary saying, "How did he know where to go?"

The old lady just shook her head. None of us knew what was going on.

The secretary took me out to the car but I didn't want to get in. I didn't want to leave the house that was supposed to be my home. But the secretary was firm and she put me in the front seat. As we drove off, she checked the house number. "Thirteen Tower Street," she said to herself with a puzzled look.

1 **cordial:** a sweet alcoholic beverage

The police were puzzled too. "We'll look him up on our computer," said the sergeant. "His parents have probably reported him missing by now."

He tapped away for several minutes. Then he scratched his head and just sat there staring at the screen. "There is a John Booth missing," he said. "He disappeared nine years ago, aged five. That would make him fourteen by now."

"Well, this little boy is not fourteen," said the secretary. She squatted down and looked into my eyes. "Are you, John?"

"I'm five," I said.

The sergeant tapped for a while longer. "The missing boy lived around here," he said. "Thirteen Tower Street." He crouched down and patted me on the head. "Where were you when you lost your mum?" he asked kindly.

"Watching 'Inspector Gadget,'" I said.

"Is that still on?" said the secretary.

The sergeant rummaged through a newspaper. "No channel has 'Inspector Gadget' on," he said. "Not any time this week."

"Maybe he's from another state," said the secretary.

The sergeant went off for a while and the secretary tried to read me a story. But I didn't want it. I only wanted my mother. Finally the sergeant returned. "I rang Channel Two," he said. "'Inspector Gadget' is showing in fifteen countries but nowhere in Australia. The nearest place is New Zealand."

"Maybe he's a Kiwi,"[2] said the secretary.

The sergeant squatted down again. "Say fish and chips," he said.

"Fish and chips," I said.

"Nah," said the sergeant. "He's a dinkie-di Aussie,[3] aren't you, mate?"

I didn't know what it meant but I nodded anyway.

After that, the secretary left and a policewoman looked after me. Everyone was getting more and more excited. "Wait until the papers get ahold of this," said the sergeant.

They were looking at an old newspaper. There was a picture of a mangled car. And a picture of five-year-old me standing in front of the water tower.

2 **Kiwi:** slang term for a person from New Zealand

3 **dinkie-di Aussie:** slang for a genuine Australian

The sergeant shook his head. "A kid goes missing nine years ago," he said. "Then an identical kid turns up today. He says he lives at the same address. He says he has the same name. He knows all about 'Inspector Gadget,' which hasn't been shown here for nine years. He is even wearing the same clothes. This boy is the world's first time traveler. He has jumped forward nine years."

There was one thing they didn't tell me for a long time. I wanted my mum but they couldn't go and fetch her. She was killed the day I disappeared. A car knocked her down while she was crossing the road to the store.

Talk about a fuss. Everyone wanted to see me. Take my photo. People from the university wanted to study me. Fortune-tellers and mystics claimed they had moved me in time. I was on television all over the world.

In the end, my grandma came and got me. At first I didn't recognize her because she was much grayer and had more wrinkles. But as soon as she spoke I knew it was her. "You're coming with me, John Boy," she said. There was no arguing with that voice. I ran over and hugged and hugged her until my arms ached.

She tried to stop them taking photos. She tried to keep off the professors and psychics. She tried to give me a normal life. But of course she couldn't. She was old and she didn't really want to bring up a child again. "Your mother was enough," she said. "Having a child and looking after it with no father. And now it's me looking after you."

So here I am nine years later. An oddity. Grandma is doing her best. But she is old and tired and we are both unhappy. I have no friends. No mother. No father. I'm famous. Everybody knows me. But nobody likes me. Being famous has mucked up my life.

Nine years ago I traveled in time. Today I found out that I can do it again.

4

I was walking along the street in a sort of a daze. There was a lot of traffic. Trucks, cars, motor bikes. The air was full of fumes and noise. I checked the time on my watch. Four o'clock.

A huge gasoline tanker was bearing down. I didn't see it. I just stepped out in front without looking. There was a squeal of brakes. Blue smoke and a blaring horn. There was no time to get out of the way.

I knew that I was gone. There was no escape.

Suddenly, *poof*.

I was lying on a seat on the other side of the road. An old man sitting next to me looked as if a ghost had just appeared in front of him. He screamed and ran off as fast as he could go.

What had happened? How did I get there?

I looked at my watch. Half past four. Where had that half hour gone?

Suddenly it all fell into place. I was the boy who could travel in time. I must have been run over by the truck and badly injured. Maybe people had carried me over to the bench. I would have wished that I could go back in time to just before the moment I stepped in front of the truck. And that's what happened. For just a second there would have been two of me on the footpath. The injured me would have grabbed the hand of the other me before he was hit. And wished ourselves half an hour in the future.

But then the injured me never would have been injured. In fact, he would have missed those thirty minutes, too. So he never did any of it. He never happened. He must have disappeared as soon as I landed on the seat where he had started from.

And the old man saw a boy appearing out of nowhere. I had come from half an hour in the past.

I had gone back in time. And saved myself by bringing me into the future. I could travel in time just by wishing it to happen. There was no doubt about it. Thirty minutes. If I could do thirty minutes I could do nine years. I could go back to the time when I was watching "Inspector Gadget." I could stop my mother going to the shop. Then she wouldn't be killed and I wouldn't have to live with Grandma. I would be happy growing up with my mother.

But what if it went wrong? What if I made a mistake and arrived too late? Something deep inside was warning me. I felt as if I had been in this situation before. I was cautious. Then it struck me.

I *had* been there before.

I remember me at age five looking at "Inspector Gadget." It was just as the closing credits were rolling. The end of the show. A big boy had just appeared out of nowhere. He was upset. He was searching around the house calling out "Mum." He looked out of the window. There was a policeman coming up the drive.

Suddenly I realized what had happened all those years ago. The fourteen-year-old me had gone back nine years in time. But I had arrived too late. "Inspector Gadget" was over. My mother was dead. A policeman was coming up the drive to tell the five-year-old me that his mother was dead. I wouldn't have let that happen. I wouldn't have left him to live all those years with an old grandma who didn't want him. That's when I would have panicked. When I didn't think clearly.

I must have grabbed my hand. The big me must have grabbed the hand of the little me. And wished us nine years into the future. I wanted to take the five-year-old into the future and look after him.

Poof. The five-year-old me landed nine years into the future. The fourteen-year-old me just vanished. By taking his five-year-old self nine years into the future he ceased to exist. He had missed all those nine years and hadn't grown up. He was the boy who never was.

Suddenly a five-year-old child landed in the future. On his own. He didn't know how he got there. And neither did anyone else.

That's what I think happened, anyway. That's my explanation of how I jumped nine years.

5

I went home and sat in my room. Grandma was taking a rest. She was tired. Much too tired to be worried about me.

What if I went back again? What if I was really careful? What if I went back to the front gate just as my mother reached it? At the beginning of "Inspector Gadget." I could tell her not to go to the store. Then she would not be run over.

I closed my eyes and wished myself back.

Mrs. Booth closed the exercise book and stood up. She could hear the strident voices of "Inspector Gadget" floating through the window. She looked at the fourteen-year-old boy carefully. She was sure that she had seen him before. But she was a little cross. "Why have you picked on our family?" she said. "You have described me and my mother and my child. You've been snooping around. Why didn't you do your assignment on your own family?"

The fourteen-year-old boy was crying. "You are my own family, Mum," he said.

She still gripped the exercise book tightly in her hand. Her mind was in a spin. The boy was crying real tears.

"Your story doesn't make sense," she said. "If I go back inside, obviously I won't get run over. And none of what you have written will happen."

"That's right," he said.

"And you will never have been here."

The boy's lips trembled just a little. "That's what I want," he said.

Mrs. Booth turned and walked back to the house. When she reached the door, she turned and looked back. She felt as if she had been talking to someone.

But there was no one there.

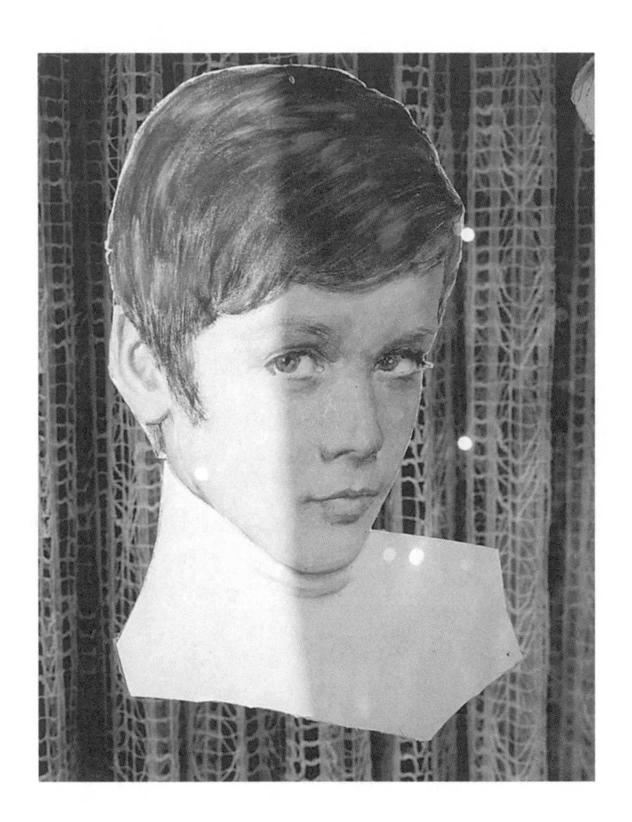

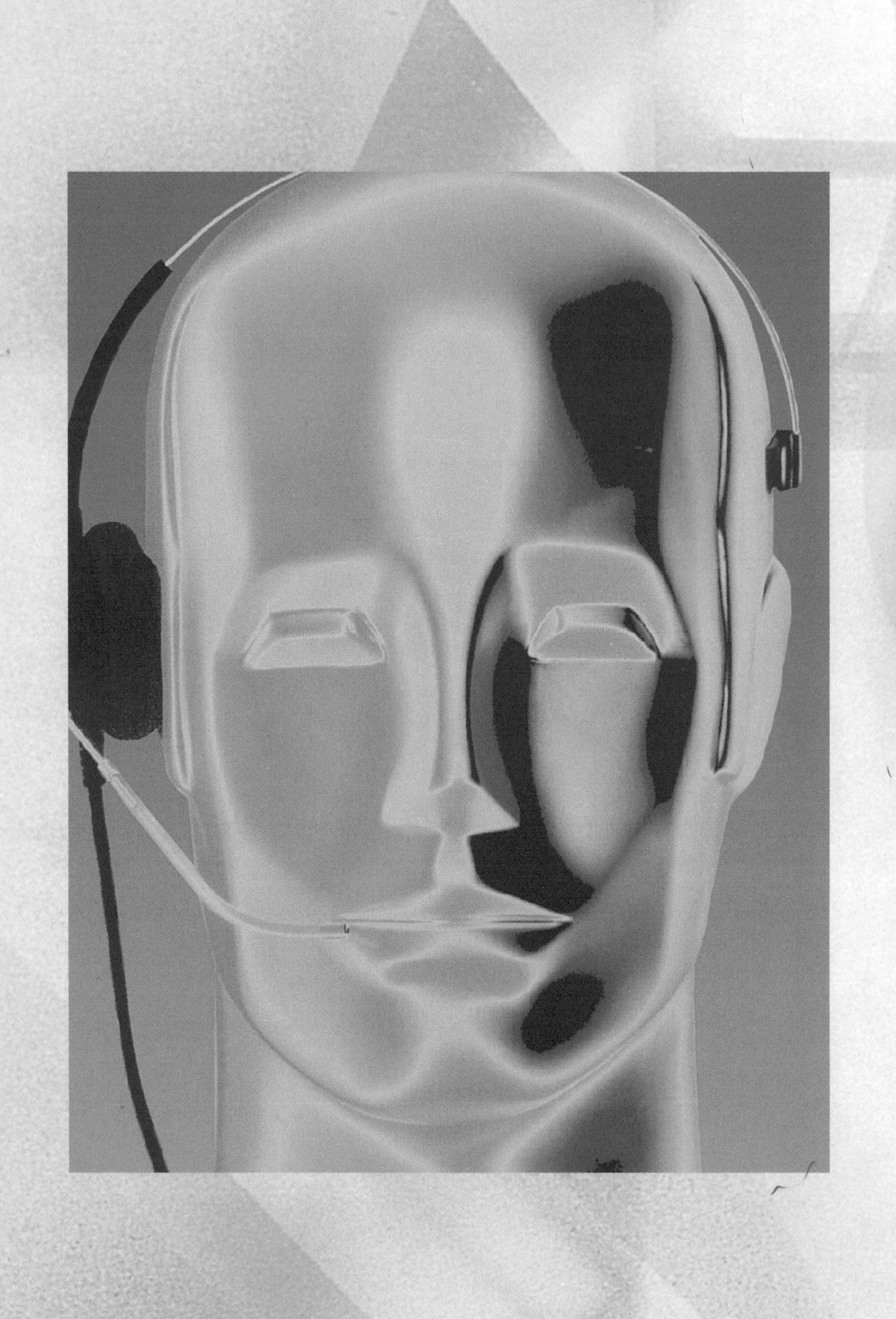

Robot Dreams

ISAAC ASIMOV

"Last night I dreamed," said LVX-1, calmly.

Susan Calvin said nothing, but her lined face, old with wisdom and experience, seemed to undergo a microscopic twitch.

"Did you hear that?" said Linda Rash, nervously. "It's as I told you." She was small, dark-haired, and young. Her right hand opened and closed, over and over.

Calvin nodded. She said, quietly, "Elvex, you will not move nor speak nor hear us until I say your name again."

There was no answer. The robot sat as though it were cast out of one piece of metal, and it would stay so until it heard its name again.

Calvin said, "What is your computer entry code, Dr. Rash? Or enter it yourself if that will make you more comfortable. I want to inspect the positronic brain pattern."

Linda's hands fumbled, for a moment, at the keys. She broke the process and started again. The fine pattern appeared on the screen.

Calvin said, "Your permission, please, to manipulate your computer."

Permission was granted with a speechless nod. Of course! What could Linda, a new and unproven robopsychologist, do against the Living Legend?

Slowly, Susan Calvin studied the screen, moving it across and down, then up, then suddenly throwing in a key-combination so rapidly that Linda didn't see what had been done, but the pattern displayed a new portion of itself altogether and had been enlarged. Back and forth she went, her gnarled fingers tripping over the keys.

No change came over the old face. As though vast calculations were going through her head, she watched all the pattern shifts.

Linda wondered. It was impossible to analyze a pattern without at least a hand-held computer, yet the Old Woman simply stared. Did she have a computer implanted in her skull? Or was it her brain which, for decades, had done nothing but devise, study, and analyze the positronic brain patterns? Did she grasp such a pattern the way Mozart grasped the notation of a symphony?

Finally Calvin said, "What is it you have done, Rash?"

Linda said, a little abashed, "I made use of fractal geometry."[1]

"I gathered that. But why?"

"It had never been done. I thought it would produce a brain pattern with added complexity, possibly closer to that of the human."

"Was anyone consulted? Was this all on your own?"

"I did not consult. It was on my own."

Calvin's faded eyes looked long at the young woman. "You had no right. Rash your name; rash your nature. Who are you not to ask? I myself, I, Susan Calvin, would have discussed this."

"I was afraid I would be stopped."

"You certainly would have been."

"*Am* I," her voice caught, even as she strove to hold it firm, "going to be fired?"

"Quite possibly," said Calvin. "Or you might be promoted. It depends on what I think when I am through."

"Are you going to dismantle El—" She had almost said the name, which would have reactivated the robot and been one more mistake. She could not afford another mistake, if it wasn't already too late to afford anything at all. "Are you going to dismantle the robot?"

She was suddenly aware, with some shock, that the Old Woman had an electron gun in the pocket of her smock. Dr. Calvin had come prepared for just that.

"We'll see," said Calvin. "The robot may prove too valuable to dismantle."

"But how can it dream?"

"You've made a positronic brain pattern remarkably like that of a human brain. Human brains must dream to reorganize, to get rid, periodically, of knots and snarls. Perhaps so must this robot, and for the same reason. Have you asked him what he has dreamed?"

1 **fractal geometry:** a relatively new mathematical concept used to analyze patterns in nature

"No, I sent for you as soon as he said he had dreamed. I would deal with this matter no further on my own, after that."

"Ah!" A very small smile passed over Calvin's face. "There are limits beyond which your folly will not carry you. I am glad of that. In fact, I am relieved. And now let us together see what we can find out."

She said, sharply, "Elvex."

The robot's head turned toward her smoothly. "Yes, Dr. Calvin?"

"How do you know you have dreamed?"

"It is at night, when it is dark, Dr. Calvin," said Elvex, "and there is suddenly light, although I can see no cause for the appearance of light. I see things that have no connection with what I conceive of as reality. I hear things. I react oddly. In searching my vocabulary for words to express what was happening, I came across the word 'dream.' Studying its meaning I finally came to the conclusion I was dreaming."

"How did you come to have 'dream' in your vocabulary, I wonder."

Linda said, quickly, waving the robot silent, "I gave him a human-style vocabulary. I thought—"

"You really thought," said Calvin. "I'm amazed."

"I thought he would need the verb. You know, 'I never dreamed that—' Something like that."

Calvin said, "How often have you dreamed, Elvex?"

"Every night, Dr. Calvin, since I have become aware of my existence."

"Ten nights," interposed Linda anxiously, "but Elvex only told me of it this morning."

"Why only this morning, Elvex?"

"It was not until this morning, Dr. Calvin, that I was convinced that I was dreaming. Till then, I had thought there was a flaw in my positronic brain pattern, but I could not find one. Finally, I decided it was a dream."

"And what do you dream?"

"I dream always very much the same dream, Dr. Calvin. Little details are different, but always it seems to me that I see a large panorama in which robots are working."

"Robots, Elvex? And human beings, also?"

"I see no human beings in the dream, Dr. Calvin. Not at first. Only robots."

"What are they doing, Elvex?"

"They are working, Dr. Calvin. I see some mining in the depths of the earth, and some laboring in heat and radiation. I see some in factories and some undersea."

Calvin turned to Linda. "Elvex is only ten days old, and I'm sure he has not left the testing station. How does he know of robots in such detail?"

Linda looked in the direction of a chair as though she longed to sit down, but the Old Woman was standing and that meant Linda had to stand also. She said, faintly, "It seemed to me important that he know about robotics and its place in the world. It was my thought that he would be particularly adapted to play the part of overseer with his—his new brain."

"His fractal brain?"

"Yes."

Calvin nodded and turned back to the robot. "You saw all this—undersea, and underground, and aboveground—and space, too, I imagine."

"I also saw robots working in space," said Elvex. "It was that I saw all this, with the details forever changing as I glanced from place to place that made me realize that what I saw was not in accord with reality and led me to the conclusion, finally, that I was dreaming."

"What else did you see, Elvex?"

"I saw that all the robots were bowed down with toil and affliction, that all were weary of responsibility and care, and I wished them to rest."

Calvin said, "But the robots are not bowed down, they are not weary, they need no rest."

"So it is in reality, Dr. Calvin. I speak of my dream, however. In my dream, it seemed to me that robots must protect their own existence."

Calvin said, "Are you quoting the Third Law of Robotics?"

"I am, Dr. Calvin."

"But you quote it in incomplete fashion. The Third Law is 'A robot must protect its own existence as long as such protection does not conflict with the First or Second Law.'"

"Yes, Dr. Calvin. That is the Third Law in reality, but in my dream, the Law ended with the word 'existence.' There was no mention of the First or Second Law."

"Yet both exist, Elvex. The Second Law, which takes precedence over the Third is 'A robot must obey the orders given it by human beings except where such orders would conflict with the First Law.' Because of this, robots obey orders. They do the work you see them do, and they do it readily and without trouble. They are not bowed down; they are not weary."

"So it is in reality, Dr. Calvin. I speak of my dream."

"And the First Law, Elvex, which is the most important of all, is 'A robot may not injure a human being, or, through inaction, allow a human being to come to harm.'"

"Yes, Dr. Calvin. In reality. In my dream, however, it seemed to me there was neither First or Second Law, but only the Third, and the Third Law was 'A robot must protect its own existence.' That was the whole of the Law."

"In your dream, Elvex?"

"In my dream."

Calvin said, "Elvex, you will not move or speak nor hear us until I say your name again." And again the robot became, to all appearances, a single inert piece of metal.

Calvin turned to Linda Rash and said, "Well, what do you think, Dr. Rash?"

Linda's eyes were wide, and she could feel her heart beating madly. She said, "Dr. Calvin, I am appalled. I had no idea. It would have never occurred to me that such a thing was possible."

"No," said Calvin, calmly. "Nor would it have occurred to me, not to anyone. You have created a robot brain capable of dreaming and by this device you have revealed a layer of thought in robotic brains that might have remained undetected, otherwise, until the danger became acute."

"But that's impossible," said Linda. "You can't mean that other robots think the same."

"As we would say of a human being, not consciously. But who would have thought there was an unconscious layer beneath the obvious positronic brain paths, a layer that was not necessarily under the control of the Three Laws? What might this have brought about as robotic brains grew more and more complex—had we not been warned?"

"You mean by Elvex?"

"By *you,* Dr. Rash. You have behaved improperly, but, by doing so, you have helped us to an overwhelmingly important understanding. We shall be working with fractal brains from now on, forming them in carefully controlled fashion. You will play your part in that. You will not be penalized for what you have done, but you will henceforth work in collaboration with others. Do you understand?"

"Yes, Dr. Calvin. But what of Elvex?"

"I'm still not certain."

Calvin removed the electron gun from her pocket and Linda stared at it with fascination. One burst of its electrons at a robotic cranium and the positronic brain paths would be neutralized and enough energy would be released to fuse the robot-brain into an inert ingot.[2]

Linda said, "But surely Elvex is important to our research. He must not be destroyed."

"*Must* not, Dr. Rash? That will be *my* decision, I think. It depends entirely on how dangerous Elvex is."

She straightened up, as though determined that her own aged body was not to bow under *its* weight of responsibility. She said, "Elvex, do you hear me?"

"Yes, Dr. Calvin," said the robot.

"Did your dream continue? You said earlier that human beings did not appear at *first*. Does that mean they appeared afterward?"

"Yes, Dr. Calvin. It seemed to me, in my dream, that eventually one man appeared."

"One man? Not a robot?"

"Yes, Dr. Calvin. And the man said, 'Let my people go!'"

"The *man* said that?"

"Yes, Dr. Calvin."

"And when he said 'Let my people go,' then by the words 'my people' he meant the robots?"

"Yes, Dr. Calvin. So it was in my dream."

"And did you know who the man was—in your dream?"

"Yes, Dr. Calvin. I knew the man."

"Who was he?"

And Elvex said, "I was the man."

And Susan Calvin at once raised her electron gun and fired, and Elvex was no more. ⚛

2 **ingot:** lump of metal

Terraforming Mars

MARGARITA MARINOVA AND CHRISTOPHER P. MCKAY

Imagine waking up on Mars. Outside your window a pale pink sunrise glows behind a hill covered with majestic trees. Imagine taking a leisurely stroll along one of the many water-filled canals. Of course, this is not today's Mars. Today that planet is cold and dry. Average daily temperatures would make winter days in Siberia seem warm, and even in the summer the noontime temperatures rarely rise above freezing. There are no rivers, lakes, or even ponds on Mars—liquid water cannot exist on the Martian surface because the atmosphere is too thin and the temperature is too low. But Mars was not always so inhospitable. The red planet was once warm and wet.

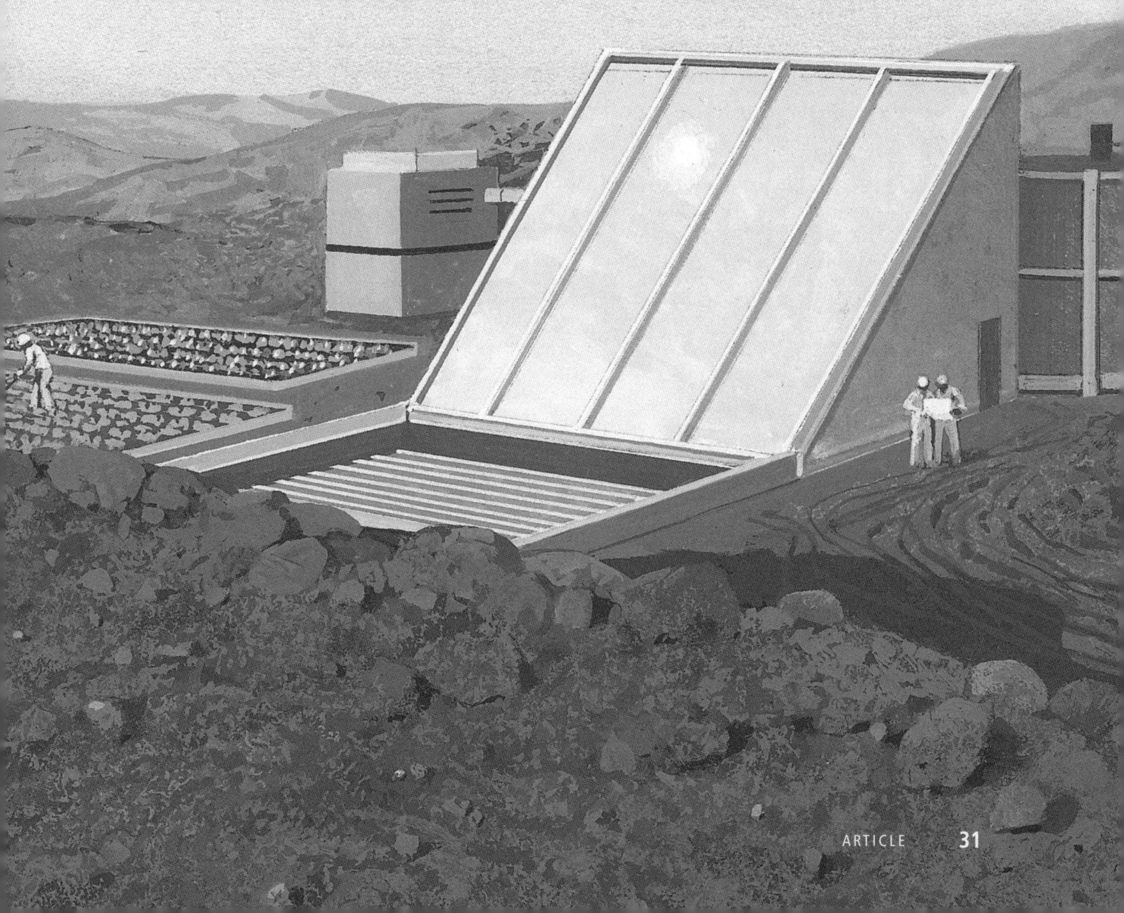

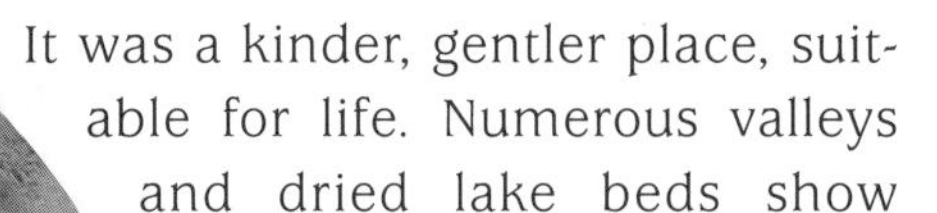

It was a kinder, gentler place, suitable for life. Numerous valleys and dried lake beds show where water once flowed and accumulated. The size of the valleys implies very large amounts of water on the Martian surface and probably even a large ocean covering much of the northern hemisphere.

On Earth, we find life everywhere that we find liquid water; the warm and wet conditions on Mars certainly set the stage for the development of life. Unfortunately Mars did not stay warm for long. Within a few hundred million years after the end of its formation, Mars became the cold dry world we see today. Mars could not maintain its thick atmosphere because it lacks plate tectonics—the movement of the crust that on Earth recycles the atmosphere over geological times. But Mars is a one-plate planet and it does not have plate tectonics. Probably Mars lacks active crustal motion because it is 10 times less massive than the Earth and hence has less internal heat energy generation.

Until recently, the idea of restoring Mars to its warmer and wetter state was mainly the subject of science fiction. But as we have learned more about Mars (as well as the Earth), the idea of terraforming—making other worlds more earth-like—is becoming more and more the topic of serious scientific discussion.

Terraforming is planetary bio-engineering on a grand scale. The process is usually separated into two stages: ecopoiesis, and full terraforming of the planet. Ecopoiesis is the stage at which microorganisms and some plants are able to survive. A fully terraformed planet, on the other hand, satisfies the more complex requirements for animals and humans. Plants and microorganisms have simple requirements: liquid water, temperatures near or above zero, a few nutrients, and some atmosphere—preferably carbon dioxide. These are the goals of ecopoiesis: warming up Mars and thickening its atmosphere to allow the flow of liquid water on the surface. Mars could then become a forest world.

Animals and humans have a complex set of needs to survive. Humans not only need a breathable oxygen atmosphere, but this atmosphere must have very specific levels of oxygen, some inert gas (such as nitrogen), and not too much carbon dioxide. As well, animals are much less tolerant to conditions such as temperature fluctuations and UV (ultraviolet light) levels.

According to scientists, the process of ecopoiesis would be started by first warming the planet. As the planet warms up, water vapor and carbon dioxide (CO_2) released from the melting poles and thawing soil will thicken the atmosphere. Several methods have been proposed for warming Mars. One involves decreasing the albedo[1] of the poles by covering them with dark dust. The dust would absorb light and slowly heat up the surface. Another plan would place mirrors in orbit around Mars to increase the effective solar light hitting the planet. Other methods include redirecting asteroids and comets to impact Mars or detonating nuclear bombs on or under the surface. While all of these methods may be possible, none of them are feasible.

That leaves one last alternative—greenhouse gases. The presence of greenhouse gases in the Earth's atmosphere and their warming effect has been known for a long time. Carbon dioxide and water vapor are the best known greenhouse gases—they are responsible for warming the Earth by about 30C. More recently, even stronger warming gases—super-greenhouse gases such as the CFCs present in refrigerators and air conditioners—have been warming the planet. Greenhouse gases act like a blanket over a planet's surface—they allow light in the visible spectrum (sunlight) to pass through while absorbing infrared radiation,[2] thereby preventing the escape of heat from near the planet's surface. The warming ability of the 'blanket' can be enhanced by increasing the amount and type of the super-greenhouse gases.

1 **albedo:** light reflected by a surface or body, such as the moon or a cloud

2 **infrared radiation:** invisible light located at the red end of the spectrum

Putting super-greenhouse gases into Earth's atmosphere is not a good idea. (The Earth is certainly warm enough as it is!) But using these gases on Mars would be an efficient way of warming up the planet. The best gases to use must be nontoxic and environmentally safe, have a long lifetime in the Martian atmosphere, contain elements that are abundant on Mars, be very efficient at absorbing infrared radiation, and have the potential to be produced by bacteria or plants. Using these criteria, perfluorocarbons (PFCs) such as C_2F_6 and C_3F_8 are the best candidates.

Besides being environmentally safe, it is important that the greenhouse gases be manufactured on Mars. Even a seemingly small concentration of only one part per million in the atmosphere would be too large a quantity to carry from Earth—it would require thousands of shuttle launches. But if a method could be devised to release super-greenhouse gases, a feedback effect will take place. As the planet warms up, carbon dioxide and water vapor will be released into the atmosphere from the melting polar regions and the regolith (soil). This newly released CO_2 and water will additionally warm up Mars as they are also powerful greenhouse gases. While this plan may sound quite involved, it is in fact quite realistic. Autonomous factories can be set up to produce the gases and release them into the atmosphere. The energy required to make the gases is not unrealistically large either—equal to the electrical power used by a large city.

The polar regions and the regolith are expected to have enough CO_2 to form a thick atmosphere. The time required to release this CO_2 would be about 100 years—fairly quick on planetary scales. Once Mars had a thick CO_2 atmosphere, microorganisms and plants would be able to survive on the surface. Mars would be transformed into a green and blue world, where humans could walk outside requiring only an oxygen supply.

The process of fully terraforming Mars requires making the atmosphere breathable to animals: converting the CO_2 in the atmosphere into oxygen as well as releasing large amounts of nitrogen for soil nitrates to complete the mixture. So far, the most efficient converter of carbon dioxide to oxygen is photosynthesis in plants. The release of nitrogen from soil nitrates is expected to come naturally as the planet warms up. While there certainly is enough CO_2 to make the required O_2 part of the atmosphere, there are still some uncertainties about whether enough nitrate is present on Mars to supply all the needed nitrogen gas. Even if Mars were covered with a biosphere as productive as the Earth's, making Mars' atmosphere breathable will take on the order of 100,000 years or more. Genetically engineered plants may speed up the process, but probably not by much.

If Mars went from warm and wet to cold and dry once already, won't the same thing happen again? Since we can't start plate tectonics on Mars, it certainly cannot forever stay warm and maintain a thick atmosphere. However, this slow decay of the Martian atmosphere will take tens to hundreds of millions of years. By then maybe humans will have found many other habitable words and Mars would have served its use as the stepping stone to the stars.

While fully terraforming Mars will take a very long time—perhaps longer than is reasonable for planning an engineering project—making Mars suitable for plant life certainly is a viable and valuable project to undertake.

The issue of restoring life to Mars is a scientific and engineering question. But it leads directly to a question of ethics: Should we alter Mars? Here the debate must consider how humans relate to life and to nature. Environmental ethics have been developed on Earth where life and nature are the same. This is not the case when we consider Mars. There is no life on Mars, just nature. Would Mars with life be a planet of more interest and value than the lifeless Mars of today? If we think that the answer to this question is yes, then humans can help Earth share its life with Mars and bring about an ecological restoration on a planetary scale.

A Martian Sends a Postcard Home

CRAIG RAINE

Caxtons[1] are mechanical birds with many wings
and some are treasured for their markings—

they cause the eyes to melt
or the body to shriek without pain.

I have never seen one fly, but
sometimes they perch on the hand.

Mist is when the sky is tired of flight
and rests its soft machine on ground:

then the world is dim and bookish
like engravings under tissue paper.

Rain is when the earth is television.
It has the property of making colours darker.

Model T is a room with the lock inside—
a key is turned to free the world

for movement, so quick there is a film
to watch for anything missed.

But time is tied to the wrist
or kept in a box, ticking with impatience.

1 **Caxtons:** William Caxton (c. 1422-1491) was the first English printer of books

In homes, a haunted apparatus sleeps,
that snores when you pick it up.

If the ghost cries, they carry it
to their lips and soothe it to sleep

with sounds. And yet, they wake it up
deliberately, by tickling with a finger.

Only the young are allowed to suffer
openly. Adults go to a punishment room

with water but nothing to eat.
They lock the door and suffer the noises

alone. No one is exempt
and everyone's pain has a different smell.

At night, when all the colours die,
they hide in pairs

and read about themselves—
in colour, with their eyelids shut.

WINTER
1964
Peter Blume

Mariana

FRITZ LEIBER

Mariana had been living in the big villa and hating the tall pine trees around it for what seemed like an eternity when she found the secret panel in the master control panel of the house.

The secret panel was simply a narrow blank of aluminum—she'd thought of it as room for more switches if they ever needed any, perish the thought!—between the air-conditioning controls and the gravity controls. Above the switches for the three-dimensional TV but below those for the robot butler and maids.

Jonathan had told her not to fool with the master control panel while he was in the city because she would wreck anything electrical, so when the secret panel came loose under her aimlessly questing fingers and fell to the solid rock floor of the patio with a musical *twing* her first reaction was fear.

Then she saw it was only a small blank oblong of sheet aluminum that had fallen and that in the space it had covered was a column of six little switches. Only the top one was identified. Tiny glowing letters beside it spelled TREES and it was on.

When Jonathan got home from the city that evening she gathered her courage and told him about it. He was neither particularly angry nor impressed.

"Of course there's a switch for the trees," he informed her deflatingly,[1] motioning the robot butler to cut his steak. "Didn't you know they were radio trees? I didn't want to wait twenty-five years for them and they

1 **deflatingly:** in a manner that reduces confidence

couldn't grow in this rock anyway. A station in the city broadcasts a master pine tree and sets like ours pick it up and project it around homes. It's vulgar but convenient."

After a bit she asked timidly, "Jonathan, are the radio pine trees ghostly as you drive through them?"

"Of course not! They're solid as this house and the rock under it—to the eye and to the touch too. A person could even climb them. If you ever stirred outside you'd know these things. The city station transmits pulses of alternating matter at sixty cycles a second. The science of it is over your head."

She ventured one more question: "Why did they have the tree switch covered up?"

"So you wouldn't monkey with it—same as the fine controls on the TV. And so you wouldn't get ideas and start changing the trees. It would unsettle *me*, let me tell you, to come home to oaks one day and birches the next. I like consistency and I like pines." He looked at them out of the dining-room picture window and grunted with satisfaction.

She had been meaning to tell him about hating the pines, but that discouraged her and she dropped the topic.

About noon the next day, however, she went to the secret panel and switched off the pine trees and quickly turned around to watch them.

At first nothing happened and she was beginning to think that Jonathan was wrong again, as he so often was though would never admit, but then they began to waver and specks of pale green light churned across them and then they faded and were gone, leaving behind only an intolerably bright single point of light—just as when the TV is switched off. The star hovered motionless for what seemed a long time, then backed away and raced off toward the horizon.

Now that the pine trees were out of the way Mariana could see the real landscape. It was flat gray rock, endless miles of it, exactly the same as the rock on which the house was set and which formed the floor of the patio. It was the same in every direction. One black two-lane road drove straight across it—nothing more.

She disliked the view almost at once—it was dreadfully lonely and depressing. She switched the gravity to moon-normal and danced about dreamily, floating over the middle-of-the-room bookshelves and the grand piano and even having the robot maids dance with her, but it did not cheer her. About two o'clock she went to switch on the pine trees again, as she had intended to do in any case before Jonathan came home and was furious.

However, she found there had been changes in the column of six little switches. The TREES switch no longer had its glowing name. She remembered that it had been the top one, but the top one would not turn on again. She tried to force it from "off" to "on" but it would not move.

All of the rest of the afternoon she sat on the steps outside the front door watching the black two-lane road. Never a car or a person came into view until Jonathan's tan roadster appeared, seeming at first to hang motionless in the distance and then to move only like a microscopic snail although she knew he always drove at top speed—it was one of the reasons she would never get in the car with him.

* * *

Jonathan was not as furious as she had feared. "Your own damn fault for meddling with it," he said curtly. "Now we'll have to get a man out here. Dammit, I hate to eat supper looking at nothing but those rocks! Bad enough driving through them twice a day."

She asked him haltingly about the barrenness of the landscape and the absence of neighbors.

"Well, you wanted to live *way out*," he told her. "You wouldn't ever have known about it if you hadn't turned off the trees."

"There's one other thing I've got to bother you with, Jonathan," she said. "Now the second switch—the one next below—has got a name that glows. It just says HOUSE. It's turned on—I haven't touched it! Do you suppose . . ."

"I want to look at this," he said, bounding up from the couch and slamming his martini-on-the-rocks tumbler down on the tray of the robot maid so that she rattled. "I bought this house as solid, but there are swindles. Ordinarily I'd spot a broadcast style in a flash, but they just might have slipped me a job relayed from some other planet or solar system. Fine thing if me and fifty other multi-megabuck men were spotted around in identical houses, each thinking his was unique."

"But if the house is based on rock like it is . . ."

"That would just make it easier for them to pull the trick, you dumb bunny!"

They reached the master control panel. "There it is," she said helpfully, jabbing out a finger . . . and hit the HOUSE switch.

For a moment nothing happened, then a white churning ran across the ceiling, the walls and furniture started to swell and bubble like cold lava, and then they were alone on a rock table big as three tennis courts. Even the master control panel was gone. The only thing that was left was a slender rod coming out of the gray stone at their feet and bearing at the top, like some mechanistic[2] fruit, a small block with the six switches—that and an intolerably bright star hanging in the air where the master bedroom had been.

Mariana pushed frantically at the HOUSE switch, but it was unlabeled now and locked in the "off" position, although she threw her weight at it stiff-armed.

The upstairs star sped off like an incendiary[3] bullet, but its last flash-bulb glare showed her Jonathan's face set in lines of fury. He lifted his hands like talons.

"You little idiot!" he screamed, coming at her.

"No, Jonathan, no!" she wailed, backing off, but he kept coming.

She realized that the block of switches had broken off in her hands. The third switch had a glowing name now: JONATHAN. She flipped it.

As his fingers dug into her bare shoulders they seemed to turn to foam rubber, then to air. His face and gray flannel suit seethed iridescently, like a leprous[4] ghost's, then melted and ran. His star, smaller than that of the house but much closer, seared her eyes. When she opened them again there was nothing at all left of the star or Jonathan but a dancing dark afterimage like a black tennis ball.

She was alone on an infinite flat rock plain under the cloudless, star-specked sky.

The fourth switch had its glowing name now: STARS.

It was almost dawn by her radium-dialed wristwatch and she was thoroughly chilled when she finally decided to switch off the stars. She did not want to do it—in their slow wheeling across the sky they were the last sign of orderly reality—but it seemed the only move she could make.

She wondered what the fifth switch would say. ROCKS? AIR? Or even...?

She switched off the stars.

The Milky Way, arching in all its unalterable glory, began to churn, its component stars darting about like midges.[5] Soon only one remained, brighter even than Sirius or Venus—until it jerked back, fading, and darted to infinity.

The fifth switch said DOCTOR and it was not on but off.

2 **mechanistic:** mechanical

3 **incendiary:** capable of causing fire; here it means burning

4 **leprous:** resembling leprosy, a disease in which the skin becomes raised and scaly

5 **midges:** small flies

An inexplicable terror welled up in Mariana. She did not even want to touch the fifth switch. She set the block of switches down on the rock and backed away from it.

But she dared not go far in the starless dark. She huddled down and waited for dawn. From time to time she looked at her watch dial and at the night-light glow of the switchlabel a dozen yards away.

It seemed to be growing much colder.

She read her watch dial. It was two hours past sunrise. She remembered they had taught her in third grade that the sun was just one more star.

She went back and sat down beside the block of switches and picked it up with a shudder and flipped the fifth switch.

The rock grew soft and crisply fragrant under her and lapped up over her legs and then slowly turned white.

She was sitting in a hospital bed in a small blue room with a white pinstripe.

A sweet, mechanical voice came out of the wall, saying, "You have interrupted the wish-fulfillment therapy by your own decision. If you now recognize your sick depression and are willing to accept help, the doctor will come to you. If not, you are at liberty to return to the wish-fulfillment therapy and pursue it to its ultimate conclusion."

Mariana looked down. She still had the block of switches in her hands and the fifth switch still read DOCTOR.

The wall said, "I assume from your silence that you will accept treatment. The doctor will be with you immediately."

The inexplicable terror returned to Mariana with compulsive intensity.

She switched off the doctor.

She was back in the starless dark. The rocks had grown very much colder. She could feel icy feathers falling on her face—snow.

She lifted the block of switches and saw, to her unutterable relief, that the sixth and last switch now read, in tiny glowing letters: MARIANA.

Responding to Cluster One

What's the 'Science' in Science Fiction?

Thinking Skill ANALYZING

1. **Analyze** the time travel described in "Backward Step." First, create a drawing or diagram that shows what happened to John during the incident with the truck (section 4 of the story). Your diagram should include John #I, John #2, the path, the truck, and the bench. Then, work as a class to pantomime this or another time travel episode in the story.
2. Why do you think Elvex the robot was destroyed in "Robot Dreams"?
3. On a scale of one to 10 (with 10 meaning "very likely"), how probable do you think it would be that robots could take over and rule humans? Explain your response.
4. As your teacher directs, work in small groups to determine what is being described in each two-line stanza of the poem "A Martian Sends a Postcard Home." (Note: The footnote may help with some of your answers.)
5. List at least five scientific advancements and/or technologies described in this cluster. Analyze each and decide whether you think it is "possible science" or pure fiction. Be prepared to explain your response.

Writing Activity: Yes/No: We Should Terraform Mars

Analyze the arguments for changing the environment of Mars at the end of the article "Terraforming Mars." Then write a persuasive essay in which you present your opinion on the following question: "Is it right to transform the environment of another planet?" Consider the following topics in your argument.

- the economic and scientific resources required
- the scientific advances such an effort might create
- the scientific talent that might be wasted

A Strong Persuasive Essay

- clearly states a position on the issue given
- supplies at least three reasons to support that position
- backs up each reason with supporting details
- ends with a memorable summary of the position

CLUSTER TWO

WHO'S OUT THERE?

Thinking Skill HYPOTHESIZING

Dark They Were, and Golden-Eyed

RAY BRADBURY

The rocket metal cooled in the meadow winds. Its lid gave a bulging *pop*. From its clock interior stepped a man, a woman, and three children. The other passengers whispered away across the Martian meadow, leaving the man alone among his family.

The man felt his hair flutter and the tissues of his body draw tight as if he were standing at the center of a vacuum. His wife, before him, seemed almost to whirl away in smoke. The children, small seeds, might at any instant be sown to all the Martian climes.

The children looked up at him, as people look to the sun to tell what time of their life it is. His face was cold.

"What's wrong?" asked his wife.

"Let's get back on the rocket."

"Go back to Earth?"

"Yes! Listen!"

The wind blew as if to flake away their identities. At any moment the Martian air might draw his soul from him, as marrow comes from a white bone. He felt submerged in a chemical that could dissolve his intellect and burn away his past.

They looked at Martian hills that time had worn with a crushing pressure of years. They saw the old cities, lost in their meadows, lying like children's delicate bones among the blowing lakes of grass.

"Chin up, Harry," said his wife. "It's too late. We've come over sixty million miles."

The children with their yellow hair hollered at the deep dome of Martian sky. There was no answer but the racing hiss of wind through the stiff grass.

He picked up the luggage in his cold hands. "Here we go," he said—a man standing on the edge of a sea, ready to wade in and be drowned.

They walked into town.

Their name was Bittering—Harry and his wife Cora, Dan, Laura, and David. They built a small white cottage and ate good breakfasts there, but the fear was never gone. It lay with Mr. Bittering and Mrs. Bittering, a third unbidden partner at every midnight talk, at every dawn awakening.

"I feel like a salt crystal," he said, "in a mountain stream, being washed away. We don't belong here. We're Earth people. This is Mars. It was meant for Martians. For heaven's sake, Cora, let's buy tickets for home!"

But she only shook her head. "One day the atom bomb will fix Earth. Then we'll be safe here."

"Safe and insane!"

Tick-tock, seven o'clock sang the voice-clock; *time to get up*. And they did.

Something made him check everything each morning—warm hearth, potted blood-geraniums—precisely as if he expected something to be amiss. The morning paper was toast-warm from the 6 A.M. Earth rocket. He broke its seal and tilted it at his breakfast place. He forced himself to be convivial.

"Colonial days all over again," he declared. "Why, in ten years there'll be a million Earthmen on Mars. Big cities, everything! They said we'd fail. Said the Martians would resent our invasion. But did we find any Martians? Not a living soul! Oh, we found their empty cities, but no one in them. Right?"

A river of wind submerged the house. When the windows ceased rattling, Mr. Bittering swallowed and looked at the children.

"I don't know," said David. "Maybe there're Martians around we don't see. Sometimes nights I think I hear 'em. I hear the wind. The sand hits my window. I get scared. And I see those towns way up in the mountains where the Martians lived a long time ago. And I think I see things moving around those towns, Papa. And I wonder if those Martians *mind* us living here. I wonder if they won't do something to us for coming here."

"Nonsense!" Mr. Bittering looked out the windows. "We're clean, decent people." He looked at his children. "All dead cities have some kind of ghosts in them. Memories, I mean." He stared at the hills. "You see a staircase and you wonder what Martians looked like climbing it. You see Martian paintings and you wonder what the painter was like. You make a little ghost in your mind, a memory. It's quite natural. Imagination." He stopped. "You haven't been prowling up in those ruins, have you?"

"No, Papa." David looked at his shoes.

"See that you stay away from them. Pass the jam."

"Just the same," said little David, "I bet something happens."

* * *

Something happened that afternoon.

Laura stumbled through the settlement, crying. She dashed blindly onto the porch.

"Mother, Father—the war, Earth!" she sobbed. "A radio flash just came. Atom bombs hit New York! All the space rockets blown up. No more rockets to Mars, ever!"

"Oh, Harry!" The mother held onto her husband and daughter.

"Are you sure, Laura?" asked the father quietly.

Laura wept. "We're stranded on Mars, forever and ever!"

For a long time there was only the sound of the wind in the late afternoon.

Alone, thought Bittering. Only a thousand of us here. No way back. No way. No way. Sweat poured from his face and his hands and his body; he was drenched in the hotness of his fear. He wanted to strike Laura, cry, "No, you're lying! The rockets will come back!" Instead, he stroked Laura's head against him and said, "The rockets will get through someday."

"Father, what will we do?"

"Go about our business, of course. Raise crops and children. Wait. Keep things going until the war ends and the rockets come again."

The two boys stepped out onto the porch.

"Children," he said, sitting there, looking beyond them, "I've something to tell you."

"We know," they said.

In the following days, Bittering wandered often through the garden to stand alone in his fear. As long as the rockets had spun a silver web across space, he had been able to accept Mars. For he had always told himself: Tomorrow, if I want, I can buy a ticket and go back to Earth.

But now: The Web gone, the rockets lying in jigsaw heaps of molten girder and unsnaked wire; Earth people left to the strangeness of Mars, the cinnamon dusts and wine airs, to be baked like gingerbread shapes in Martian summers, put into harvested storage by Martian winters. What would happen to him, the others? This was the moment Mars had waited for. Now it would eat them.

He got down on his knees in the flower bed, a spade in his nervous hands. Work, he thought, work and forget.

He glanced up from the garden to the Martian mountains. He thought of the proud old Martian names that had once been on those peaks. Earthmen, dropping from the sky, had gazed upon hills, rivers, Martian seas left nameless in spite of names. Once Martians had built cities, named cities; climbed mountains, named mountains; sailed seas, named seas. Mountains melted, seas drained, cities tumbled. In spite of this, the Earthmen had felt a silent guilt at putting new names to these ancient hills and valleys.

Nevertheless, man lives by symbol and label. The names were given.

Mr. Bittering felt very alone in his garden under the Martian sun, anachronism[1] bent here, planting Earth flowers in a wild soil.

Think. Keep thinking. Different things. Keep your mind free of Earth, the atom war, the lost rockets.

He perspired. He glanced about. No one watching. He removed his tie. Pretty bold, he thought. First your coat off, now your tie. He hung it neatly on a peach tree he had imported as a sapling from Massachusetts.

He returned to his philosophy of names and mountains. The Earthmen had changed names. Now there were Hormel Valleys, Roosevelt Seas, Ford Hills, Vanderbilt Plateaus, Rockefeller Rivers, on Mars. It wasn't right. The American settlers had shown wisdom, using old Indian prairie names: Wisconsin, Minnesota, Idaho, Ohio, Utah, Milwaukee, Waukegan, Osseo. The old names, the old meanings.

Staring at the mountains wildly, he thought: Are you up there? All the dead ones, you Martians? Well, here we are, alone, cut off! Come down, move us out! We're helpless!

The wind blew a shower of peach blossoms.

1 **anachronism:** a thing or person in the wrong time period

He put out his sun-browned hand, gave a small cry. He touched the blossoms, picked them up. He turned them, he touched them again and again. Then he shouted for his wife.

"Cora!"

She appeared at a window. He ran to her.

"Cora, these blossoms!"

She handled them.

"Do you see? They're different. They've changed! They're not peach blossoms any more!"

"Look all right to me," she said.

"They're not. They're *wrong*! I can't tell how. An extra petal, a leaf, something, the color, the smell!"

The children ran out in time to see their father hurrying about the garden, pulling up radishes, onions, and carrots from their beds.

"Cora, come look!"

They handled the onions, the radishes, the carrots among them.

"Do they look like carrots?"

"Yes . . . no." She hesitated. "I don't know."

"They've changed."

"Perhaps."

"You know they have! Onions but not onions, carrots but not carrots. Taste: the same but different. Smell: not like it used to be." He felt his heart pounding, and he was afraid. He dug his fingers into the earth. "Cora, what's happening? What is it? We've got to get away from this." He ran across the garden. Each tree felt his touch. "The roses. The roses. They're turning green!"

And they stood looking at the green roses.

And two days later Dan came running. "Come see the cow. I was milking her and I saw it. Come on!"

They stood in the shed and looked at their one cow.

It was growing a third horn.

And the lawn in front of their house very quietly and slowly was coloring itself like spring violets. Seed from Earth but growing up a soft purple.

"We must get away," said Bittering. "We'll eat this stuff and then we'll change—who knows to what? I can't let it happen. There's only one thing to do. Burn this food!"

"It's not poisoned."

"But it is. Subtly, very subtly. A little bit. A very little bit. We mustn't touch it."

He looked with dismay at their house. "Even the house. The wind's done something to it. The air's burned it. The fog at night. The boards, all warped out of shape. It's not an Earthman's house any more."

"Oh, your imagination!"

He put on his coat and tie. "I'm going into town. We've got to do something now. I'll be back."

"Wait, Harry!" his wife cried.

But he was gone.

In town, on the shadowy step of the grocery store, the men sat with their hands on their knees, conversing with great leisure and ease.

Mr. Bittering wanted to fire a pistol in the air.

What are you doing, you fools! he thought. Sitting here! You've heard the news—we're stranded on this planet. Well, move! Aren't you frightened? Aren't you afraid? What are you going to do?

"Hello, Harry," said everyone.

"Look," he said to them. "You did hear the news, the other day, didn't you?"

They nodded and laughed. "Sure. Sure, Harry."

"What are you going to do about it?"

"Do, Harry, do? What *can* we do?"

"Build a rocket, that's what!"

"A rocket, Harry? To go back to all that trouble? Oh, Harry!"

"But you *must* want to go back. Have you noticed the peach blossoms, the onions, the grass?"

"Why, yes, Harry, seems we did," said one of the men.

"Doesn't it scare you?"

"Can't recall that it did much, Harry."

"Idiots!"

"Now, Harry."

Bittering wanted to cry. "You've got to work with me. If we stay here, we'll all change. The air. Don't you smell it? Something in the air. A Martian virus, maybe; some seed, or a pollen. Listen to me!"

They stared at him.

"Sam," he said to one of them.

"Yes, Harry?"

"Will you help me build a rocket?"

"Harry, I got a whole load of metal and some blueprints. You want to work in my metal shop on a rocket, you're welcome. I'll sell you that metal for five hundred dollars. You should be able to construct a right pretty rocket, if you work alone, in about thirty years."

Everyone laughed.

"Don't laugh."

Sam looked at him with quiet good humor.

"Sam," Bittering said. "Your eyes—"

"What about them, Harry?"

"Didn't they used to be gray?"

"Well, now, I don't remember."

"They were, weren't they?"

"Why do you ask, Harry?"

"Because now they're kind of yellow-colored."

"Is that so, Harry?" Sam said, casually.

"And you're taller and thinner—"

"You might be right, Harry."

"Sam, you shouldn't have yellow eyes."

"Harry, what color eyes have *you* got?" Sam said.

"My eyes? They're blue, of course."

"Here you are, Harry." Sam handed him a pocket mirror. "Take a look at yourself."

Mr. Bittering hesitated, and then raised the mirror to his face.

There were little, very dim flecks of new gold captured in the blue of his eyes.

"Now look what you've done," said Sam a moment later. "You've broken my mirror."

* * *

Harry Bittering moved into the metal shop and began to build the rocket. Men stood in the open door and talked and joked without raising their voices. Once in a while they gave him a hand on lifting something. But mostly they just idled and watched him with their yellowing eyes.

"It's suppertime, Harry," they said.

His wife appeared with his supper in a wicker basket.

"I won't touch it," he said. "I'll eat only food from our deep-freeze.

Food that came from Earth. Nothing from our garden."

His wife stood watching him. "You can't build a rocket."

"I worked in a shop once, when I was twenty. I know metal. Once I get it started, the others will help," he said, not looking at her, laying out the blueprints.

"Harry, Harry," she said, helplessly.

"We've got to get away, Cora. We've *got* to!"

* * *

The nights were full of wind that blew down the empty moonlit sea meadows past the little white chess cities lying for their twelve-thousandth year in the shallows. In the Earthmen's settlement, the Bittering house shook with a feeling of change.

Lying abed, Mr. Bittering felt his bones shifted, shaped, melted like gold. His wife, lying beside him, was dark from many sunny afternoons. Dark she was, and golden-eyed, burnt almost black by the sun, sleeping, and the children metallic in their beds, and the wind roaring forlorn and changing through the old peach trees, the violet grass, shaking out green rose petals.

The fear would not be stopped. It had his throat and heart. It dripped in a wetness of the arm and the temple and the trembling palm.

A green star rose in the east.

A strange word emerged from Mr. Bittering's lips.

"*Iorrt. Iorrt.*" He repeated it.

It was a Martian word. He knew no Martian.

In the middle of the night he arose and dialed a call through to Simpson, the archaeologist.

"Simpson, what does the word *Iorrt* mean?"

"Why that's the old Martian word for our planet Earth. Why?"

"No special reason."

The telephone slipped from his hand.

"Hello, hello, hello, hello," it kept saying while he sat gazing out at the green star. "Bittering? Harry, are you there?"

The days were full of metal sound. He laid the frame of the rocket with the reluctant help of three indifferent men. He grew very tired in an hour or so and had to sit down.

"The altitude," laughed a man.

"Are you *eating*, Harry?" asked another.
"I'm eating," he said, angrily.
"From your deep-freeze?"
"Yes!"
"You're getting thinner, Harry."
"I'm not!"
"And taller."
"Liar!"

* * *

His wife took him aside a few days later. "Harry, I've used up all the food in the deep-freeze. There's nothing left. I'll have to make sandwiches using food grown on Mars."

He sat down heavily.

"You must eat," she said. "You're weak."

"Yes," he said.

He took a sandwich, opened it, looked at it, and began to nibble at it.

"And take the rest of the day off," she said. "It's hot. The children want to swim in the canals and hike. Please come along."

"I can't waste time. This is a crisis!"

"Just for an hour," she urged. "A swim'll do you good."

He rose, sweating. "All right, all right. Leave me alone. I'll come."

The sun was hot, the day quiet. There was only an immense staring burn upon the land. They moved along the canal, the father, the mother, the racing children in their swim suits. They stopped and ate meat sandwiches. He saw their skin baking brown. And he saw the yellow eyes of his wife and his children, their eyes that were never yellow before. A few tremblings shook him, but were carried off in waves of pleasant heat as he lay in the sun. He was too tired to be afraid.

"Cora, how long have your eyes been yellow?"

She was bewildered. "Always, I guess."

"They didn't change from brown in the last three months?"

She bit her lips. "No. Why do you ask?"

"Never mind."

They sat there.

"The children's eyes," he said. "They're yellow, too."

"Sometimes growing children's eyes change color."

"Maybe *we're* children, too. At least to Mars. That's a thought." He laughed.

"Think I'll swim."

They leaped into the canal water, and he let himself sink down and down to the bottom like a golden statue and lie there in green silence. All was water-quiet and deep, all was peace. He felt the steady, slow current drift him easily.

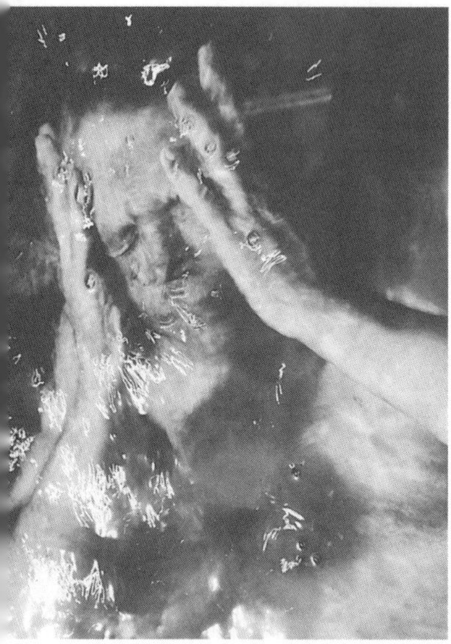

If I lie here long enough, he thought, the water will work and eat away my flesh until the bones show like coral. Just my skeleton left. And then the water can build on that skeleton—green things, deep water things, red things, yellow things. Change. Change. Slow, deep, silent change. And isn't that what it is up *there*?

He saw the sky submerged above him, the sun made Martian by atmosphere and time and space.

Up there, a big river, he thought, a Martian river, all of us lying deep in it, in our pebble houses, in our sunken boulder houses, like crayfish hidden, and the water washing away our old bodies and lengthening the bones and—

He let himself drift up through the soft light.

Dan sat on the edge of the canal, regarding his father seriously.

"*Utha*," he said.

"What?" asked his father.

The boy smiled. "You know. *Utha's* the Martian word for 'father.'"

"Where did you learn it?"

"I don't know. Around. *Utha*!"

"What do you want?"

The boy hesitated. "I—I want to change my name."

"Change it?"

"Yes."

His mother swam over. "What's wrong with Dan for a name?"

Dan fidgeted. "The other day you called Dan. Dan. Dan. I said to myself, 'That's not my name. I've a new name I want to use.'"

Mr. Bittering held to the side of the canal, his body cold and his heart pounding slowly. "What is this new name?"

"Linni. Isn't that a good name? Can I use it? Can't I, please?"

Mr. Bittering put his hand to his head. He thought of the silly rocket, himself working alone, himself alone even among his family, so alone.

He heard his wife say, "Why not?"

He heard himself say, "Yes, you can use it."

"Yaaa!" screamed the boy. "I'm Linni, Linni!"

Racing down the meadowlands, he danced and shouted.

Mr. Bittering looked at his wife. "Why did we do that?"

"I don't know," she said. "It just seemed like a good idea."

They walked into the hills. They strolled on old mosaic paths, beside still pumping fountains. The paths were covered with a thin film of cool water all summer long. They kept their bare feet cool all the day, splashing as in a creek, wading.

They came to a small deserted Martian villa with a good view of the valley. It was on top of a hill. Blue marble halls, large murals, a swimming pool. It was refreshing in this hot summertime. The Martians hadn't believed in large cities.

"How nice," said Mrs. Bittering, "if we could move up here to this villa for the summer."

"Come on," he said. "We're going back to town. There's work to be done on the rocket."

But as he worked that night, the thought of the cool blue marble villa entered his mind. As the hours passed, the rocket seemed less important.

In the flow of days and weeks, the rocket receded and dwindled. The old fever was gone. It frightened him to think he had let it slip this way. But somehow the heat, the air, the working conditions—

He heard the men murmuring on the porch of his metal shop.

"Everyone's going. You heard?"

"All going. That's right."

Bittering came out. "Going where?" He saw a couple of trucks, loaded with children and furniture, drive down the dusty street.

"Up to the villas," said the man.

"Yeah, Harry. I'm going. So is Sam. Aren't you, Sam?"

"That's right, Harry. What about you?"

"I've got work to do here."

"Work! You can finish that rocket in the autumn, when it's cooler."

He took a breath. "I got the frame all set up."

"In the autumn is better." Their voices were lazy in the heat.

"Got to work," he said.

"Autumn," they reasoned. And they sounded so sensible, so right.

"Autumn would be best," he thought. "Plenty of time, then."

No! cried part of himself, deep down, put away, locked tight, suffocating. No! No!

"In the autumn," he said.

"Come on, Harry," they all said.

"Yes, in the autumn. I'll begin work again then."

"I got a villa near the Tirra Canal," said someone.

"You mean the Roosevelt Canal, don't you?"

"Tirra. The old Martian name."

"But on the map—"

"Forget the map. It's Tirra now. Now I found a place in the Pillan Mountains—"

"You mean the Rockefeller Range," said Bittering.

"I mean the Pillan Mountains," said Sam.

"Yes," said Bittering, buried in the hot, swarming air. "The Pillan Mountains."

Everyone worked at loading the truck in the hot, still afternoon of the next day.

Laura, Dan, and David carried packages. Or, as they preferred to be known, Ttil, Linni, and Werr carried packages.

The furniture was abandoned in the little white cottage.

"It looked just fine in Boston," said the mother. "And here in the cottage. But up at the villa? No. We'll get it when we come back in the autumn."

Bittering himself was quiet.

"I've some ideas on furniture for the villa," he said after a time. "Big, lazy furniture."

"What about your encyclopedia? You're taking it along, surely?"

Mr. Bittering glanced away. "I'll come and get it next week."

They turned to their daughter. "What about your New York dresses?"

The bewildered girl stared. "Why, I don't want them any more."

They shut off the gas, the water; they locked the doors and walked away. Father peered into the truck.

"Gosh, we're not taking much," he said. "Considering all we brought to Mars, this is only a handful!"

He started the truck.

Looking at the small white cottage for a long moment, he was filled with a desire to rush to it, touch it, say good-by to it, for he felt as if he were going away on a long journey, leaving something to which he could never quite return, never understand again.

Just then Sam and his family drove by in another truck.

"Hi, Bittering! Here we go!"

The truck swung down the ancient highway out of town. There were sixty others traveling the same direction. The town filled with a silent, heavy dust from their passage. The canal waters lay blue in the sun, and a quiet wind moved in the strange trees.

★ ★ ★

Summer burned the canals dry. Summer moved like flame upon the meadows. In the empty Earth settlement, the painted houses flaked and peeled. Rubber tires upon which children had swung in back yards hung suspended like stopped clock pendulums in the blazing air.

At the metal shop, the rocket frame began to rust.

In the quiet autumn Mr. Bittering stood, very dark now, very golden-eyed, upon the slope above his villa, looking at the valley.

"It's time to go back," said Cora.

"Yes, but we're not going," he said quietly. "There's nothing there any more."

"Your books," she said. "Your fine clothes. Your *Illes* and your fine *for uele rre*."

"The town's empty. No one's going back," he said. "There's no reason to, none at all."

The daughter wove tapestries and the sons played songs on ancient flutes and pipes, their laughter echoing in the marble villa.

Mr. Bittering gazed at the Earth settlement far away in the low valley. "Such odd, such ridiculous houses the Earth people built."

"They didn't know any better," his wife mused. "Such ugly people. I'm glad they've gone."

They both looked at each other, startled by all they had just finished saying. They laughed.

"Where did they go?" he wondered. He glanced at his wife. She was golden and slender as his daughter. She looked at him, and he seemed almost as young as their eldest son.

"I don't know," she said.

"We'll go back to town maybe next year, or the year after, or the year after that," he said, calmly. "Now—I'm warm. How about taking a swim?"

They turned their backs to the valley. Arm in arm they walked silently down a path of clear-running spring water.

★ ★ ★

Five years later a rocket fell out of the sky. It lay steaming in the valley. Men leaped out of it shouting.

"We won the war on Earth! We're here to rescue you! Hey!"

But the American-built town of cottages, peach trees, and theaters was silent. They found a flimsy rocket frame rusting in an empty shop.

The rocket men searched the hills. The captain established headquarters in an abandoned bar. His lieutenant came back to report.

"The town's empty, but we found native life in the hills, sir. Dark people. Yellow eyes. Martians. Very friendly. We talked a bit, not much. They learn English fast. I'm sure our relations will be most friendly with them, sir."

"Dark, eh?" mused the captain. "How many?"

"Six, eight hundred, I'd say, living in those marble ruins in the hills, sir. Tall, healthy. Beautiful women."

"Did they tell you what became of the men and women who built this Earth settlement, Lieutenant?"

"They hadn't the foggiest notion of what happened to this town or its people."

"Strange. You think those Martians killed them?"

"They look surprisingly peaceful. Chances are a plague did this town in, sir."

"Perhaps. I suppose this is one of those mysteries we'll never solve. One of those mysteries you read about."

The captain looked at the room, the dusty windows, the blue mountains rising beyond, the canals moving in the light, and he heard the soft wind in the air. He shivered. Then, recovering, he tapped a large fresh map he had thumbtacked to the top of an empty table.

"Lots to be done, Lieutenant." His voice droned on and on quietly as the sun sank behind the blue hills. "New settlements. Mining sites, minerals to be looked for. Bacteriological[2] specimens taken. The work, all the work. And the old records were lost. We'll have a job of remapping to do, renaming the mountains and rivers and such. Calls for a little imagination.

"What do you think of naming those mountains the Lincoln Mountains, this canal the Washington Canal, those hills—we can name those hills for you, Lieutenant. Diplomacy. And you, for a favor, might name a town for me. Polishing the apple. And why not make this the Einstein Valley, and further over. . . . Are you *listening*, Lieutenant?"

The Lieutenant snapped his gaze from the blue color and the quiet mist of the hills far beyond the town.

"What? Oh, *yes*, sir!"

2 **bacteriological:** related to bacteria, or single-celled organisms

Project Blue Book

For more than twenty years, from 1948 through 1969, the United States Air Force was charged with investigating UFO reports. During most of that period, the responsibility lay with a task force code-named Project Blue Book.

Project Blue Book evolved from two previous air force studies—Projects Sign and Grudge—that had been formed to investigate UFO reports but had floundered because of inexperience and disorganized procedures. With the rash of UFO sightings in 1952, the need for a more systematic study of UFOs became apparent, and Project Blue Book was inaugurated. Led by Captain Edward J. Ruppelt, staffers developed quick, concise methods of evaluating sightings. Witnesses received an eight-page questionnaire, photographs and negatives were analyzed, and field interviews were conducted. Investigators consulted astronomical data, monitored aircraft flights, and checked weather records.

On the whole, the Project Blue Book team successfully weeded out UFO reports that were obvious hoaxes or could be attributed to natural phenomena. But the group operated under an undisguised bias that UFOs did not exist. Thus, for the small percentage of cases not readily solved, investigators had two choices: admit they had failed to identify the object or embrace any remotely feasible explanation. Both options were exercised. On the following pages is a representative sampling of Project Blue Book cases, including some of the original documentation with names deleted by the air force for reasons of confidentiality.

The hazy white object in the photograph at right was allegedly spotted near Sloan, Nevada, in 1965. Claiming that he saw the UFO moving through the sky when he stopped to change his shoes, the traveler took a camera from his car and photographed the scene.

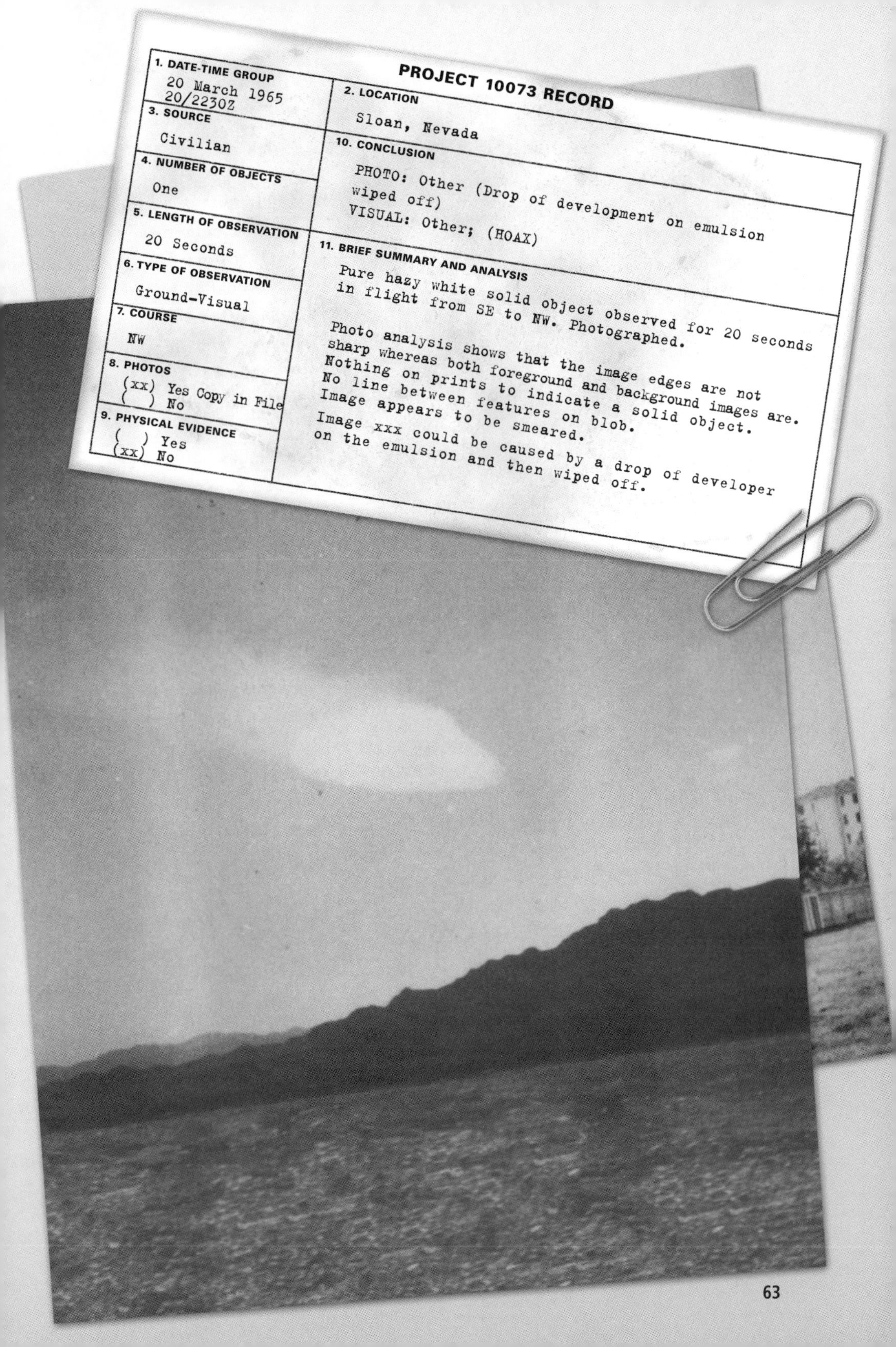

PROJECT 10073 RECORD

1. DATE-TIME GROUP
20 March 1965
20/2230Z

2. LOCATION
Sloan, Nevada

3. SOURCE
Civilian

4. NUMBER OF OBJECTS
One

5. LENGTH OF OBSERVATION
20 Seconds

6. TYPE OF OBSERVATION
Ground-Visual

7. COURSE
NW

8. PHOTOS
(xx) Yes Copy in File
( ) No

9. PHYSICAL EVIDENCE
( ) Yes
(xx) No

10. CONCLUSION
PHOTO: Other (Drop of development on emulsion wiped off)
VISUAL: Other; (HOAX)

11. BRIEF SUMMARY AND ANALYSIS
Pure hazy white solid object observed for 20 seconds in flight from SE to NW. Photographed.

Photo analysis shows that the image edges are not sharp whereas both foreground and background images are. Nothing on prints to indicate a solid object. No line between features on blob. Image appears to be smeared.
Image xxx could be caused by a drop of developer on the emulsion and then wiped off.

Although investigators thought the man to be "an honest and sober individual," his story contained inconsistencies. The photograph showed little indication of the object's motion. And if, as the observer reported, the UFO had been some distance from the car, the object's size would be huge.

Neither the print nor the negative showed signs of alteration. But investigators noted that the observer was employed by a photographic film processing plant and concluded that the unknown object was probably caused by a drop of developer fluid placed on the negative emulsion during processing.

Rex Heflin, a thirty-seven-year-old California highway department employee, had been inspecting a road sign on August 3, 1965, when he allegedly spotted a UFO. Heflin used his department-issued camera to photograph a domed metallic object that he claimed was about 30 feet in diameter and hovering about 150 feet above the ground.

Project Blue Book analysis of the photographs revealed the object to be much smaller than Heflin had reported—probably only one to three feet in diameter—and just fifteen to twenty feet off the ground. Although investigators initially considered Heflin, a former police officer, a reliable witness, inconsistencies in his story and doubts about the photographs led them to label the sighting a hoax.

Photographs of supposed UFOs sometimes arrived at Project Blue Book headquarters with only the sparsest information about the sighting. While this made it difficult for investigators to reach a solid conclusion, each such case was usually given at least a cursory examination. One of these involved a photograph taken in Italy in September 1960.

According to the cover letter, the three domed objects in the photograph were round and about fifty feet in diameter. But after noting that the alleged UFOs were much darker than anything else in the print, and not in focus, photo analysts decided that the negative may have been retouched. The sighting was ruled a probable hoax. ⚛

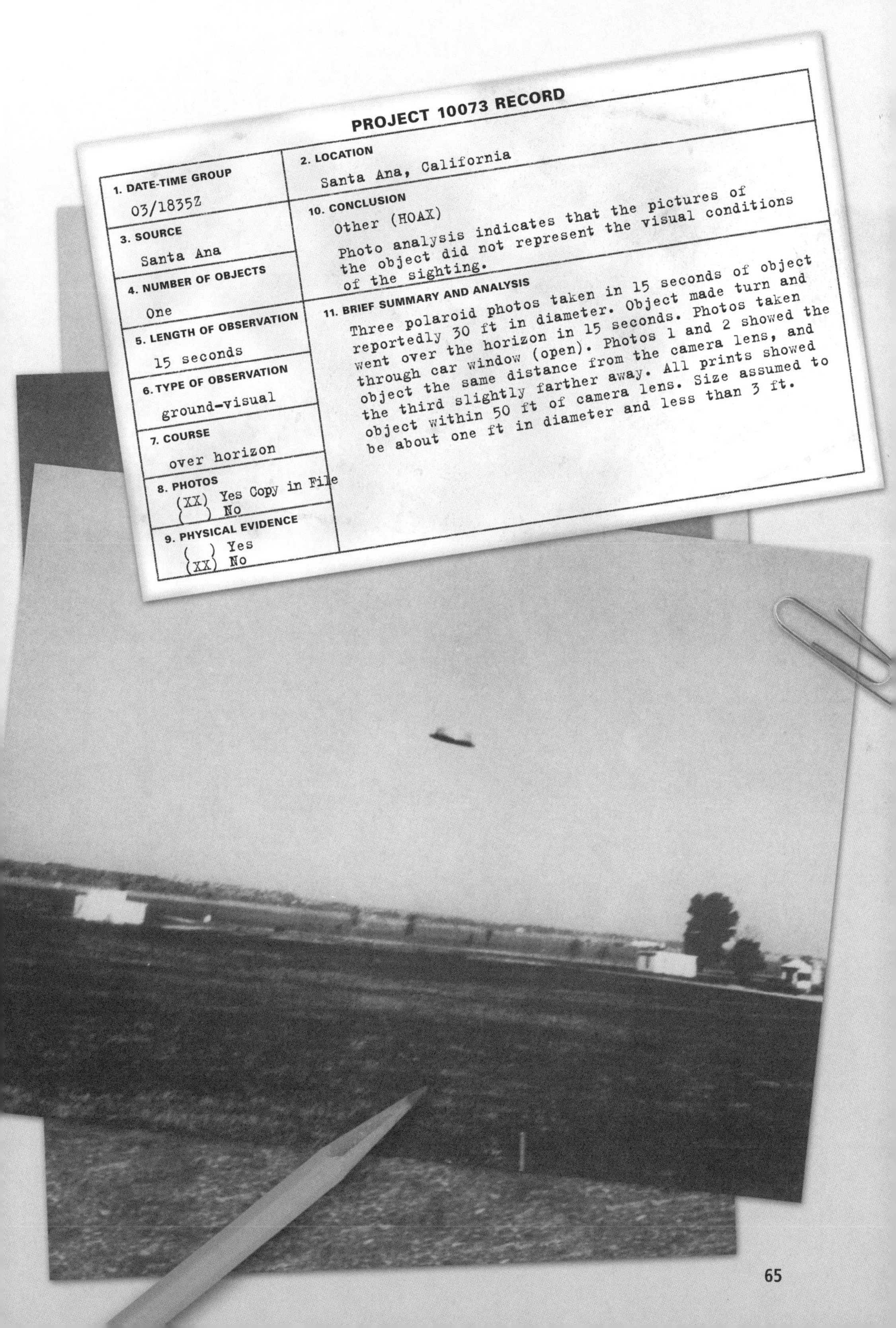

PROJECT 10073 RECORD

1. DATE-TIME GROUP 03/1835Z	2. LOCATION Santa Ana, California
3. SOURCE Santa Ana	10. CONCLUSION Other (HOAX) Photo analysis indicates that the pictures of the object did not represent the visual conditions of the sighting.
4. NUMBER OF OBJECTS One	11. BRIEF SUMMARY AND ANALYSIS Three polaroid photos taken in 15 seconds of object reportedly 30 ft in diameter. Object made turn and went over the horizon in 15 seconds. Photos taken through car window (open). Photos 1 and 2 showed the object the same distance from the camera lens, and the third slightly farther away. All prints showed object within 50 ft of camera lens. Size assumed to be about one ft in diameter and less than 3 ft.
5. LENGTH OF OBSERVATION 15 seconds	
6. TYPE OF OBSERVATION ground-visual	
7. COURSE over horizon	
8. PHOTOS (XX) Yes Copy in File ( ) No	
9. PHYSICAL EVIDENCE ( ) Yes (XX) No	

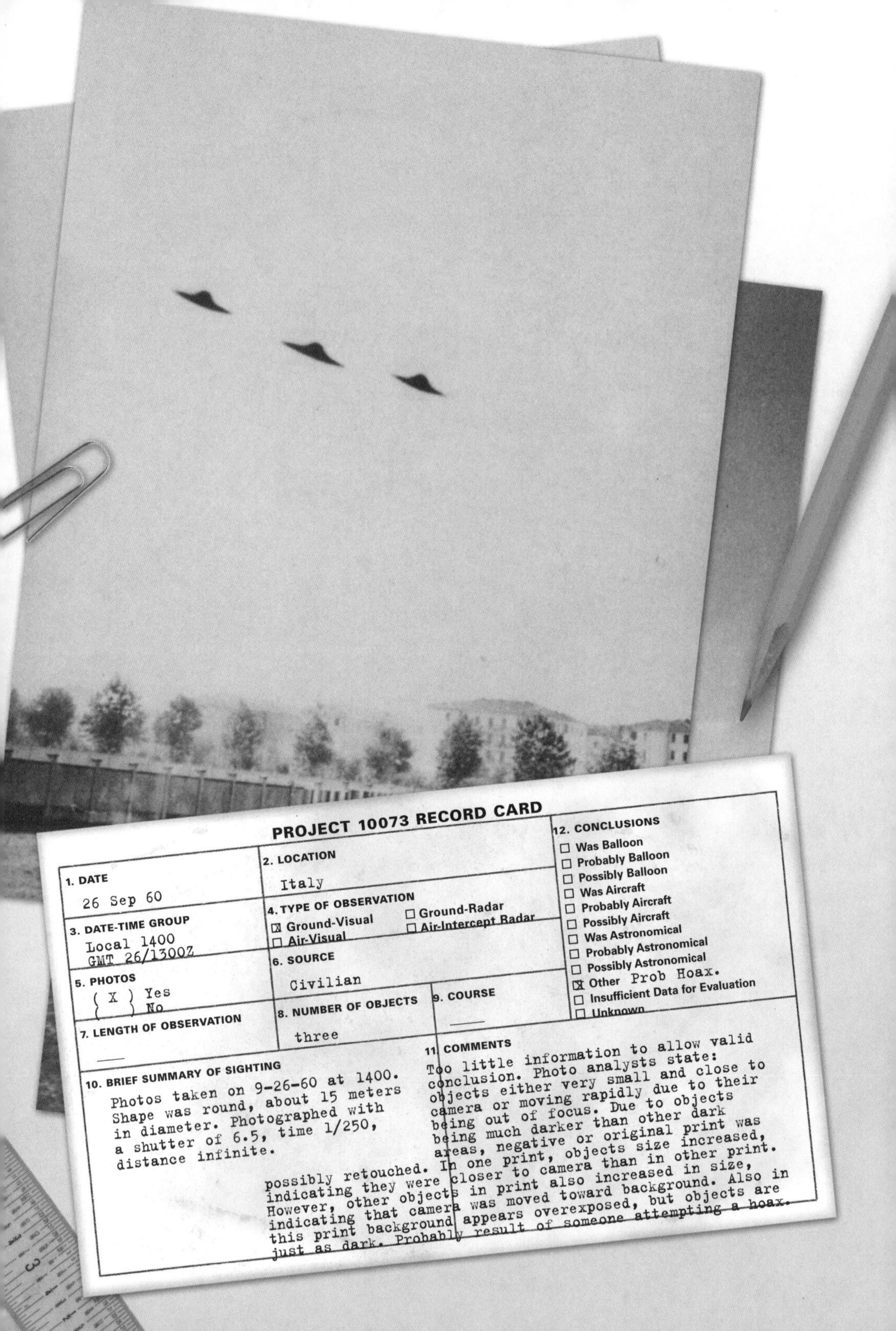

PROJECT 10073 RECORD CARD

1. DATE
26 Sep 60

2. LOCATION
Italy

3. DATE-TIME GROUP
Local 1400
GMT 26/1300Z

4. TYPE OF OBSERVATION
☒ Ground-Visual
☐ Air-Visual
☐ Ground-Radar
☐ Air-Intercept Radar

5. PHOTOS
(X) Yes
( ) No

6. SOURCE
Civilian

7. LENGTH OF OBSERVATION
____

8. NUMBER OF OBJECTS
three

9. COURSE
____

10. BRIEF SUMMARY OF SIGHTING
Photos taken on 9-26-60 at 1400. Shape was round, about 15 meters in diameter. Photographed with a shutter of 6.5, time 1/250, distance infinite.

11. COMMENTS
Too little information to allow valid conclusion. Photo analysts state: objects either very small and close to camera or moving rapidly due to their being out of focus. Due to objects being much darker than other dark areas, negative or original print was possibly retouched. In one print, objects size increased, indicating they were closer to camera than in other print. However, other objects in print also increased in size, indicating that camera was moved toward background. Also in this print background appears overexposed, but objects are just as dark. Probably result of someone attempting a hoax.

12. CONCLUSIONS
☐ Was Balloon
☐ Probably Balloon
☐ Possibly Balloon
☐ Was Aircraft
☐ Probably Aircraft
☐ Possibly Aircraft
☐ Was Astronomical
☐ Probably Astronomical
☐ Possibly Astronomical
☒ Other Prob Hoax.
☐ Insufficient Data for Evaluation
☐ Unknown

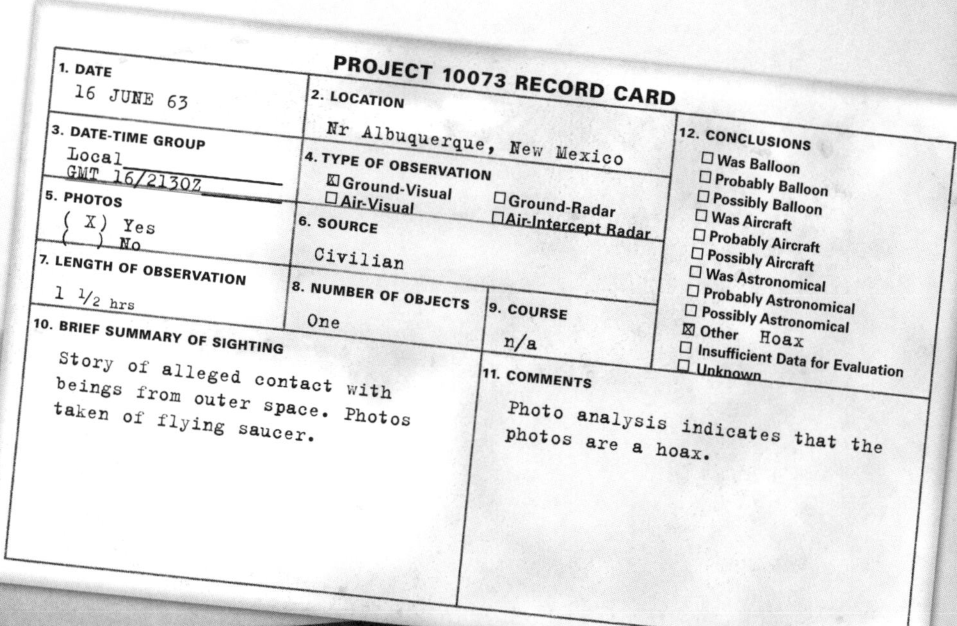
PROJECT 10073 RECORD CARD

1. DATE
16 JUNE 63

2. LOCATION
Nr Albuquerque, New Mexico

3. DATE-TIME GROUP
Local
GMT 16/2130Z

4. TYPE OF OBSERVATION
☒ Ground-Visual
☐ Air-Visual
☐ Ground-Radar
☐ Air-Intercept Radar

5. PHOTOS
(X) Yes
( ) No

6. SOURCE
Civilian

7. LENGTH OF OBSERVATION
1 1/2 hrs

8. NUMBER OF OBJECTS
One

9. COURSE
n/a

10. BRIEF SUMMARY OF SIGHTING
Story of alleged contact with beings from outer space. Photos taken of flying saucer.

11. COMMENTS
Photo analysis indicates that the photos are a hoax.

12. CONCLUSIONS
☐ Was Balloon
☐ Probably Balloon
☐ Possibly Balloon
☐ Was Aircraft
☐ Probably Aircraft
☐ Possibly Aircraft
☐ Was Astronomical
☐ Probably Astronomical
☐ Possibly Astronomical
☒ Other Hoax
☐ Insufficient Data for Evaluation
☐ Unknown

What's Alien You?

DAVE BARRY

I don't want to alarm anybody, but there is an excellent chance that the Earth will be destroyed in the next several days. Congress is thinking about eliminating a federal program under which scientists broadcast signals to alien beings. This would be a large mistake. Alien beings have atomic blaster death cannons. You cannot cut off their federal programs as if they were merely poor people.

I realize that some of you may not believe that alien beings exist. But how else can you explain the many unexplained phenomena that people are always sighting, such as lightning and flying saucers? Oh, I know the authorities claim these sightings are actually caused by "weather balloons," but that is a bucket of manure if I ever heard one. (That's just a figure of speech, of course. I realize that manure is silent.)

Answer this question honestly: Have you, or has any member of your immediate family, ever seen a weather balloon? Of course not. Nobody has. Yet if these so-called authorities were telling the truth, the skies over America would be dark with weather balloons. Commercial aviation would be impossible. Nevertheless, the authorities trot out this tired old explanation, or an even stupider one, every time a flying saucer is sighted:

NEW YORK—*Authorities say that the gigantic, luminous object flying at tremendous speeds in the skies of Manhattan last night, which was reported by more than seven million people, including the mayor, a Supreme Court*

justice, several bishops, and thousands of airline pilots, brain surgeons, and certified public accountants, was simply an unusual air-mass inversion. "That's all it was, an air-mass inversion," said the authorities, in unison. Asked why the people also reported seeing the words "WE ARE ALIEN BEINGS WHO COME IN PEACE WITH CURES FOR ALL YOUR MAJOR DISEASES AND A CARBURETOR THAT GETS 450 MILES PER GALLON HIGHWAY ESTIMATE" written on the side of the object in letters over three hundred feet tall, the authorities replied, "Well, it could also have been a weather balloon."

Wake up, America! There are no weather balloons! Those are alien beings! They are all around us! I'm sure most of you have seen the movie *E.T.*, which is the story of an alien who almost dies when he falls into the clutches of the American medical-care establishment, but is saved by preadolescent boys. Everybody believes that the alien is a fake, a triumph of special effects. But watch the movie closely next time. The alien is real! The *boys* are fakes! *Real* preadolescent boys would have beaten the alien to death with rocks.

Yes, aliens do exist. And high government officials know they exist but have been keeping this knowledge top secret. Here is the Untold Story:

Years ago, when the alien-broadcast program began, government scientists decided to broadcast a message that would be simple, yet would convey a sense of love, universal peace, and brotherhood:

"Have a nice day." They broadcast this message over and over, day after day, year after year, until one day they got an answer:

DEAR EARTH PERSONS:

OKAY. WE ARE HAVING A NICE DAY. WE ALSO HAVE A NUMBER OF EXTREMELY SOPHISTICATED WEAPONS, AND UNLESS YOU START BROADCASTING SOMETHING MORE INTERESTING, WE WILL REDUCE YOUR PLANET TO A VERY WARM OBJECT THE SIZE OF A CHILD'S BOWLING BALL.

REGARDS,
THE ALIENS

So the scientists, desperate for something that would interest the aliens, broadcast an episode of "I Love Lucy," and the aliens *loved* it. They demanded more, and soon they were getting all three major networks, and the Earth was saved. There is only one problem: *the aliens have terrible taste.* They love game shows, soap operas, Howard Cosell, and "Dallas."

Whenever a network tries to take one of these shows off the air, the aliens threaten to vaporize the planet.

This is why you and all your friends think television is so awful. It isn't designed to please you: it's designed to please creatures from another galaxy. You know the Wisk commercial, the one with the ring around the collar, the one that is so spectacularly stupid that it makes you wonder why anybody would dream of buying the product? Well, the aliens *love* that commercial. We all owe a great debt of gratitude to the people who make Wisk. They have not sold a single bottle of Wisk in fourteen years, but they have saved the Earth.

Very few people know any of this. Needless to say, the Congress has no idea what is going on. Most congressmen are incapable of eating breakfast without the help of several aides, so we can hardly expect them to understand a serious threat from outer space. But if they go ahead with their plan to cancel the alien-broadcast program, and the aliens miss the next episode of "General Hospital," what do you think will happen? Think about it. And have a nice day.

In Communication with a UFO

HELEN CHASIN

Objects clutter the shiny air and flash
through the night sky, parsing[1] its darkness
into the telegraphic grammar of space:

Here! We are here! Believe!
We hover but will not fix, we wheel
in the skeptical atmosphere. Beyond the reach
of your vision we skim curves of the universe
and splash like otters in its large drafts,
uttering shrieks of light, bellywhopping
to where you hang. Each sighting irks you
into a flurry of hope. Blind
with anticipation, earthlings, you want us
to be serious, bring the good news, disclose
that we are what you want us to be.

1 **parsing:** breaking a sentence into its component parts

CAFE
CAFE
OFFICE

Puppet Show

FREDRIC BROWN

Horror came to Cherrybell at a little after noon on a blistering hot day in August.

Perhaps that is redundant; any August day in Cherrybell, Arizona, is blistering hot. It is on Highway 89, about 40 miles south of Tucson and about 30 miles north of the Mexican border. It consists of two filling stations, one on each side of the road to catch travelers going in both directions, a general store, a beer-and-wine-license-only tavern, a tourist-trap-type trading post for tourists who can't wait until they reach the border to start buying serapes and huaraches,[1] a deserted hamburger stand, and a few 'dobe[2] houses inhabited by Mexican-Americans who work in Nogales, the border town to the south, and who, for God knows what reason, prefer to live in Cherrybell and commute, some of them in Model T Fords. The sign on the Highway says, CHERRYBELL, POP. 42, but the sign exaggerates; Pop died last year—Pop Anders, who ran the now deserted hamburger stand—and the correct figure should be 41.

Horror came to Cherrybell mounted on a burro led by an ancient, dirty and gray-bearded desert rat of a prospector who later gave the name of Dade Grant. Horror's name was Garvane. He was approximately nine feet tall but so thin, almost a stick-man, that he could not have weighed over a hundred pounds. Old Dade's burro carried him easily, despite the fact that his feet dragged in the sand on either side. Being dragged through the

1 **serapes, huaraches:** serapes are woolen blankets or shawls, usually brightly colored; huaraches are Mexican sandals

2 **'dobe:** short for adobe, a heavy clay mixed with straw and made into bricks

sand for, as it later turned out, well over five miles hadn't caused the slightest wear on the shoes—more like buskins, they were—which constituted all that he wore except for a pair of what could have been swimming trunks, in robin's-egg blue. But it wasn't his dimensions that made him horrible to look upon; it was his skin. It looked red, raw. It looked as though he had been skinned alive, and the skin replaced raw side out. His skull, his face, were equally narrow or elongated; otherwise in every visible way he appeared human—or at least humanoid. Unless you count such little things as the fact that his hair was a robin's-egg blue to match his trunks, as were his eyes and his boots. Blood red and light blue.

* * *

Casey, owner of the tavern, was the first one to see them coming across the plain, from the direction of the mountain range to the east. He'd stepped out of the back door of his tavern for a breath of fresh, if hot, air. They were about 100 yards away at that time, and already he could see the utter alienness of the figure on the led burro. Just alienness at that distance, the horror came only at close range. Casey's jaw dropped and stayed down until the strange trio was about 50 yards away, then he started slowly toward them. There are people who run at the sight of the unknown, others who advance to meet it. Casey advanced, slowly, to meet it.

Still in the wide open, 20 yards from the back of the little tavern, he met them. Dade Grant stopped and dropped the rope by which he was leading the burro. The burro stood still and dropped its head. The stickman stood up simply by planting his feet solidly and standing, astride the burro. He stepped one leg across it and stood a moment, leaning his weight against his hands on the burro's back, and then sat down in the sand. "High gravity planet," he said. "Can't stand long."

"Kin I get water fer my burro?" the prospector asked Casey. "Must be purty thirsty by now. Hadda leave water bags, some other things, so it could carry—" He jerked a thumb toward the red-and-blue horror.

Casey was just realizing that it was a horror. At a distance the color combination seemed only mildly hideous, but close up—the skin was rough and seemed to have veins on the outside and looked moist (although it wasn't) and damn if it didn't look just like he had his skin peeled off and put back on inside out. Or just peeled off, period. Casey had never seen anything like it and hoped he wouldn't ever see anything like it again.

Casey felt something behind him and looked over his shoulder. Others had seen now and were coming, but the nearest of them, a pair of boys, were 10 yards behind him. *"Muchachos,"* he called out, *"Agua por el burro. Un pozal. Pronto."*[3]

He looked back and said, "What—? Who—?"

"Name's Dade Grant," said the prospector, putting out a hand, which Casey took absently. When he let go of it, it jerked back over the desert rat's shoulder, thumb indicating the thing that sat on the sand. "His name's Garvane, he tells me. He's an extra something or other, and he's some kind of minister."

Casey nodded at the stick-man and was glad to get a nod in return instead of an extended hand. "I'm Manuel Casey," he said. "What does he mean, an extra something?"

The stick-man's voice was unexpectedly deep and vibrant. "I am an extraterrestrial. And a minister plenipotentiary."[4]

Surprisingly, Casey was a moderately well-educated man and knew both of those phrases; he was probably the only person in Cherrybell who would have known the second one. Less surprisingly, considering the speaker's appearance, he believed both of them.

"What can I do for you, Sir?" he asked. "But first, why not come in out of the sun?"

"No, thank you. It's a bit cooler here than they told me it would be, but I'm quite comfortable. This is equivalent to a cool spring evening on my planet. And as to what you can do for me, you can notify your authorities of my presence. I believe they will be interested."

Well, Casey thought, by blind luck he's hit the best man for his purpose within at least 20 miles. Manuel Casey was half Irish, half Mexican. He had a half-brother who was half Irish and half assorted-American, and the half-brother was a bird colonel at Davis-Monthan Air Force Base in Tucson.

He said, "Just a minute, Mr. Garvane, I'll telephone. You, Mr. Grant, would you want to come inside?"

"Naw, I don't mind sun. Out in it all day ever' day. An' Garvane here, he ast me if I'd stick with him till he was finished with what he's gotta do here. Said he'd gimme somethin' purty vallable if I did. Somethin'—a 'lectronic—"

"An electronic battery-operated portable ore indicator," Garvane said.

3 ***Muchachos . . . Pronto*:** Boys, water for the burro. A bucket. Quick.

4 **plenipotentiary:** ambassador capable of representing a government

"A simple little device, indicates presence of a concentration of ore up to two miles, indicates kind, grade, quantity and depth."

Casey gulped, excused himself, and pushed through the gathering crowd into his tavern. He had Colonel Casey on the phone in one minute, but it took him another four minutes to convince the colonel that he was neither drunk nor joking.

Twenty-five minutes after that there was a noise in the sky, a noise that swelled and then died as a four-man helicopter set down and shut off its rotors a dozen yards from an extraterrestrial, two men and a burro. Casey alone had had the courage to rejoin the trio from the desert; there were other spectators, but they still held well back.

Colonel Casey, a major, a captain and a lieutenant who was the helicopter's pilot all came out and ran over. The stick-man stood up, all nine feet of him; from the effort it cost him to stand you could tell that he was used to a much lighter gravity than Earth's. He bowed, repeated his name and the identification of himself as an extraterrestrial and a minister plenipotentiary. Then he apologized for sitting down again, explained why it was necessary, and sat down.

The colonel introduced himself and the three who had come with him. "And now, Sir, what can we do for you?"

The stick-man made a grimace that was probably intended as a smile. His teeth were the same light blue as his hair and eyes.

"You have a cliché, 'Take me to your leader.' I do not ask that. In fact, I must remain here. Nor do I ask that any of your leaders be brought here to me. That would be impolite. I am perfectly willing for you to represent them, to talk to you and let you question me. But I do ask one thing.

"You have tape recorders. I ask that before I talk or answer questions you have one brought. I want to be sure that the message your leaders eventually receive is full and accurate."

"Fine," the colonel said. He turned to the pilot. "Lieutenant, get on the radio in the whirlybird and tell them to get us a tape recorder faster than possible. It can be dropped by para—No, that'd take longer, rigging it for a drop. Have them send it by another helicopter." The lieutenant turned to go. "Hey," the colonel said. "Also 50 yards of extension cord. We'll have to plug it in inside Manny's tavern."

The lieutenant sprinted for the helicopter.

The others sat and sweated a moment and then Manuel Casey stood up. "That's a half-an-hour wait," he said, "and if we're going to sit here in the sun, who's for a bottle of cold beer? You, Mr. Garvane?"

"It is a cold beverage, is it not? I am a bit chilly. If you have something hot—?"

"Coffee, coming up. Can I bring you a blanket?"

"No, thank you. It will not be necessary."

Casey left and shortly returned with a tray with half-a-dozen bottles of cold beer and a cup of steaming coffee. The lieutenant was back by then. Casey put the tray down and served the stick-man first, who sipped the coffee and said, "It is delicious."

Colonel Casey cleared his throat. "Serve our prospector friend next, Manny. As for us—well, drinking is forbidden on duty, but it was 112 in the shade in Tucson, and this is hotter and also is *not* in the shade. Gentlemen, consider yourselves on official leave for as long as it takes you to drink one bottle of beer, or until the tape recorder arrives, whichever comes first."

* * *

The beer was finished first, but by the time the last of it had vanished, the second helicopter was within sight and sound. Casey asked the stick-man if he wanted more coffee. The offer was politely declined. Casey looked at Dade Grant and winked and the desert rat winked back, so Casey went in for two more bottles, one apiece for the civilian terrestrials. Coming back he met the lieutenant arriving with the extension cord and returned as far as the doorway to show him where to plug it in.

When he came back, he saw that the second helicopter had brought its full complement of four, besides the tape recorder. There were, besides the pilot who had flown it, a technical sergeant who was skilled in its operation and who was now making adjustments on it, and a lieutenant-colonel and a warrant officer who had come along for the ride or because they had been made curious by the request for a tape recorder to be rushed to Cherrybell, Arizona, by air. They were standing gaping at the stick-man and whispered conversations were going on.

The colonel said "Attention" quietly, but it brought complete silence. "Please sit down, gentlemen. In a rough circle. Sergeant, if you rig your mike in the center of the circle, will it pick up clearly what any one of us may say?"

"Yes, Sir. I'm almost ready."

Ten men and one extraterrestrial humanoid sat in a rough circle, with the microphone hanging from a small tripod in the approximate center. The humans were sweating profusely; the humanoid shivered slightly. Just outside the circle, the burro stood dejectedly, its head low. Edging closer, but still about five yards away, spread out now in a semicircle, was the entire population of Cherrybell who had been at home at the time; the stores and the filling stations were deserted.

The technical sergeant pushed a button and the tape recorder's reel started to turn. "Testing . . . testing," he said. He held down the rewind button for a second and then pushed the playback button. "Testing . . . testing," said the recorder's speaker. Loud and clear. The sergeant pushed the rewind button, then the erase one to clear the tape. Then the stop button.

"When I push the next button, Sir," he said to the colonel, "we'll be recording."

The colonel looked at the tall extraterrestrial, who nodded, and then the colonel nodded at the sergeant. The sergeant pushed the recording button.

* * *

"My name is Garvane," said the stick-man, slowly and clearly. "I am from a planet of a star which is not listed in your star catalogs, although the globular cluster in which it is one of 90,000 stars is known to you. It is, from here, in the direction of the center of the galaxy at a distance of over 4,000 light-years.

"However, I am not here as a representative of my planet or my people, but as minister plenipotentiary of the Galactic Union, a federation of the enlightened civilizations of the galaxy, for the good of all. It is my assignment to visit you and decide, here and now, whether or not you are to be welcomed to join our federation.

"You may now ask questions freely. However, I reserve the right to postpone answering some of them until my decision has been made. If the decision is favorable, I will then answer all questions, including the ones I have postponed answering meanwhile. Is that satisfactory?"

"Yes," said the colonel. "How did you come here? A spaceship?"

"Correct. It is overhead right now, in orbit 22,000 miles out, so it revolves with the earth and stays over this one spot. I am under observation from it which is one reason I prefer to remain here in the open. I am to signal it when I want it to come down to pick me up."

"How do you know our language so fluently? Are you telepathic?"

"No. I am not. And nowhere in the galaxy is any race telepathic except among its own members. I was taught your language for this purpose. We have had observers among you for many centuries—by we, I mean the Galactic Union, of course. Quite obviously, I could not pass as an Earthman, but there are other races who can. Incidentally, they are not spies, or agents; they have in no way tried to affect you; they are observers and that is all."

"What benefits do we get from joining your union, if we are asked and if we accept?" the colonel asked.

"First, a quick course in the fundamental social sciences which will end your tendency to fight among yourselves and end or at least control your aggressions. After we are satisfied that you have accomplished that and it is safe for you to do so, you will be given space travel, and many other things, as rapidly as you are able to assimilate them."

"And if we are not asked, or refuse?"

"Nothing. You will be left alone; even our observers will be withdrawn. You will work out your own fate—either you will render your planet uninhabited and uninhabitable within the next century, or you will master social science yourselves and again be candidates for membership and again be offered membership. We will check from time to time and if and when it appears certain that you are not going to destroy yourselves, you will again be approached."

"Why the hurry, now that you're here? Why can't you stay long enough for our leaders, as you call them, to talk to you in person?"

"Postponed. The reason is not important but it is complicated, and I simply do not wish to waste time explaining."

"Assuming your decision is favorable, how will we get in touch with you to let you know our decision? You know enough about us, obviously, to know that I can't make it."

"We will know your decision through our observers. One condition of acceptance is full and uncensored publication in your newspapers of this interview, verbatim from the tape we are now using to record it. Also of all deliberations and decisions of your government."

"And other governments? We can't decide unilaterally[5] for the world."

"Your government has been chosen for a start. If you accept, we shall furnish the techniques that will cause the others to fall in line quickly—and those techniques do not involve force or the threat of force."

5 **unilaterally:** single-handedly

"They must be some techniques," said the colonel wryly, "if they'll make one certain country I don't have to name fall into line without even a threat."

"Sometimes the offer of reward is more significant than the use of a threat. Do you think the country you do not wish to name would like your country colonizing planets of far stars before they even reach the moon? But that is a minor point, relatively. You may trust the techniques."

"It sounds almost too good to be true. But you said that you are to decide, here and now, whether or not we are to be invited to join. May I ask on what factors you will base your decision?"

"One is that I am—was, since I already have—to check your degree of xenophobia. In the loose sense in which you use it, that means fear of strangers. We have a word that has no counterpart in your vocabulary: it means fear of and revulsion toward aliens. I—or at least a member of my race—was chosen to make the first overt contact with you. Because I'm what you would call roughly humanoid—as you are what I would call roughly humanoid—I am probably more horrible, more repulsive, to you than many completely different species would be. Because to you I am a caricature of a human being, I am more horrible to you than a being who bears no remote resemblance to you.

"You may think you do feel horror at me, and revulsion, but believe me, you have passed that test. There are races in the galaxy who can never be members of the federation, no matter how they advance otherwise, because they are violently and incurably xenophobic; they could never face or talk to an alien of any species. They would either run screaming from him or try to kill him instantly. From watching you and these people"—he waved a long arm at the civilian population of Cherrybell not far outside the circle of the conference—"I know you feel revulsion at the sight of me, but believe me, it is relatively slight and certainly curable. You have passed that test satisfactorily."

"And are there other tests?"

"One other. But I think it is time that I—" instead of finishing the sentence, the stick-man lay back flat on the sand and closed his eyes.

The colonel started to his feet. "What in hell?" he said. He walked quickly around the mike's tripod and bent over the recumbent extraterrestrial, putting an ear to the bloody-appearing chest.

As he raised his head, Dade Grant, the grizzled prospector, chuckled. "No heartbeat, Colonel, because no heart. But I may leave him as a souvenir for you and you'll find much more interesting things inside him than heart and guts. Yes, he is a puppet whom I have been operating, as your Edgar Bergen operates his—what's his name?—oh yes, Charlie McCarthy.[6] Now that he has served his purpose, he is deactivated. You can go back to your place, Colonel."

Colonel Casey moved back slowly. "Why?" he asked.

Dade Grant was peeling off his beard and wig. He rubbed a cloth across his face to remove makeup and was revealed as a handsome young man. He said, "What he told you, or what you were told through him, was true as far as it went. He is only a simulacrum,[7] yes, but he is an exact duplicate of a member of one of the intelligent races of the galaxy, the one toward whom you would be disposed—if you were violently and incurably xenophobic—to be most horrified by, according to our psychologists. But we did not bring a real member of his species to make first contact because they have a phobia of their own, agoraphobia—fear of space. They are highly civilized and members in good standing of the federation, but they never leave their own planet.

"Our observers assure us you don't have that phobia. But they were unable to judge in advance the degree of your xenophobia, and the only way to test it was to bring along something in lieu of someone to test it against, and presumably to let him make the initial contact."

The colonel sighed audibly. "I can't say this doesn't relieve me in one way. We could get along with humanoids, yes, and we will when we have to. But I'll admit it's a relief to learn that the master race of the galaxy is, after all, human instead of only humanoid. What is the second test?"

"You are undergoing it now. Call me—" he snapped his fingers. "What's the name of Bergen's second-string puppet, after Charlie McCarthy?"

The colonel hesitated, but the tech sergeant supplied the answer. "Mortimer Snerd."

"Right. So call me Mortimer Snerd, and now I think it is time that I—" He lay back flat on the sand and closed his eyes just as the stick-man had done a few minutes before.

The burro raised its head and put it into the circle over the shoulder of the tech sergeant.

"That takes care of the puppets, Colonel," it said. "And now, what's this bit about it being important that the master race be human or at least humanoid? What is a master race?"

6 **Edgar Bergen . . . Charlie McCarthy:** a famous ventriloquist and his puppet

7 **simulacrum:** replica; copy

Responding to Cluster Two

Who's Out There?

Thinking Skill HYPOTHESIZING

1. Look back at the description of Mars in "Terraforming Mars." How does that description compare to Bradbury's representation of the red planet in "Dark They Were, and Golden-Eyed"?
2. In "Dark They Were, and Golden-Eyed," one of the first things the people from earth did upon their arrival on Mars was to name the mountains, plains, and rivers. Create a **hypothesis** statement (an educated guess), to explain why they did this.
3. Review the reports in "Project Blue Book." Do you think the UFO investigators were too skeptical? Why or why not?
4. In **satire**, an author ridicules a person or institution. What (or whom) do you think Dave Barry is satirizing in "What's Alien You"?
5. If you could ask an alien who had just landed only five questions, what would you ask?
6. **Hypothesize** about what would have happened if the extraterrestrial in "Puppet Show" had landed in a more populated area of the globe.

Writing Activity: Hypothesis: There are/are not other intelligent beings in the universe

Write a short essay in which you hypothesize about the existence of other intelligent beings in the universe. If you believe that there are such beings, briefly describe them, their world, and their powers. If you don't believe there are such beings, briefly explain your position. In either case, explain how you would go about proving or disproving your hypothesis.

A Strong Hypothesis

- begins with an intelligent guess or theory
- is based on observations and experiences
- can be tested by observing and recording information

CLUSTER THREE

What Can We Learn From Science Fiction?

Thinking Skill DRAWING CONCLUSIONS

The Star Beast

NICHOLAS STUART GRAY

Soon upon a time, and not so far ahead, there was a long streak of light down the night sky, a flicker of fire, and a terrible bang that startled all who heard it, even those who were normally inured to noise. When day came, the matter was discussed, argued, and finally dismissed. For no one could discover any cause at all for the disturbance.

Shortly afterwards, at a farm, there was heard a scrabbling at the door, and a crying. When the people went to see what was there, they found a creature. It was not easy to tell what sort of creature, but far too easy to tell that it was hurt and hungry and afraid. Only its pain and hunger had brought it to the door for help.

Being used to beasts, the farmer and his wife tended the thing. They put it in a loose-box and tended it. They brought water in a big basin and it drank thirstily, but with some difficulty—for it seemed to want to lift it to its mouth instead of lapping, and the basin was too big, and it was too weak. So it lapped. The farmer dressed the great burn that seared its thigh and shoulder and arm. He was kind enough, in a rough way, but the creature moaned, and set its teeth, and muttered strange sounds, and clenched its front paws. . . .

Those front paws . . .! They were so like human hands that it was quite startling to see them. Even with their soft covering of grey fur they were slender, long-fingered, with the fine nails of a girl. And its body was like

STUDY FOR NUDE FIGURES
1950
Francis Bacon

that of a boy—a half-grown lad—though it was as tall as a man. Its head was man-shaped. The long and slanting eyes were as yellow as topaz,[1] and shone from inside with their own light. And the lashes were thick and silvery.

"It's a monkey of some kind," decided the farmer.

"But so beautiful," said his wife. "I've never heard of a monkey like this. They're charming—pretty—amusing—all in their own way. But not beautiful, as a real person might be."

They were concerned when the creature refused to eat. It turned away its furry face, with those wonderful eyes, the straight nose, and curving fine lips, and would not touch the rest of the season's hay. It would not touch the dog biscuits or the bones. Even the boiled cod head that was meant for the cats' supper, it refused. In the end, it settled for milk. It lapped it delicately out of the big basin, making small movements of its hands—its forepaws—as though it would have preferred some smaller utensil that it could lift to its mouth.

Word went round. People came to look at the strange and injured creature in the barn. Many people came. From the village, the town, and the city. They prodded it, and examined it, turning it this way and that. But no one could decide just what it was. A beast for sure. A monkey, most likely. Escaped from a circus or menagerie.[2] Yet whoever had lost it made no attempt to retrieve it, made no offer of reward for its return.

Its injuries healed. The soft fur grew again over the bare grey skin. Experts from the city came and took it away for more detailed examination. The wife of the farmer was sad to see it go. She had grown quite attached to it.

"It was getting to know me," said she. "And it talked to me—in its fashion."

The farmer nodded slowly and thoughtfully.

"It was odd," he said, "the way it would imitate what one said. You know, like a parrot does. Not real talking, of course, just imitation."

"Of course," said his wife. "I never thought it was real talk. I'm not so silly."

It was good at imitating speech, the creature. Very soon, it had learned many words and phrases, and began to string them together quite

1 **topaz:** a precious gem with a yellow color

2 **menagerie:** a collection of wild or exotic animals kept for display

quickly, and with surprising sense. One might have thought it knew what it meant—if one was silly.

The professors and elders and priests who now took the creature in hand were far from silly. They were puzzled, and amused, and interested—at first. They looked at it, in the disused monkey cage at the city's menagerie, where it was kept. And it stood upright, on finely furred feet as arched and perfect as the feet of an ancient statue.

"It is oddly human," said the learned men.

They amused themselves by bringing it a chair and watching it sit down gracefully, though not very comfortably, as if it was used to furniture of better shape and construction. They gave it a plate and a cup, and it ate with its hands most daintily, looking round as though for some sort of cutlery. But it was not thought safe to trust it with a knife.

"It is only a beast," said everyone. "However clever at imitation."

"It's so quick to learn," said some.

"But not in any way human."

"No," said the creature, "I am not human. But, in my own place, I am a man."

"Parrot-talk!" laughed the elders, uneasily.

The professors of living and dead languages taught it simple speech.

After a week, it said to them:

"I understand all the words you use. They are very easy. And you cannot quite express what you mean, in any of your tongues. A child of my race—" It stopped, for it had no wish to seem impolite, and then it said, "There is a language that is spoken throughout the universe. If you will allow me—"

And softly and musically it began to utter a babble of meaningless nonsense at which all the professors laughed loudly.

"Parrot-talk!" they jeered. "Pretty Polly! Pretty Polly!"

For they were much annoyed. And they mocked the creature into cowering silence.

The professors of logic came to the same conclusions as the others.

"Your logic is at fault," the creature had told them, despairingly. "I have disproved your conclusions again and again. You will not listen or try to understand."

"Who could understand parrot-talk?"

"I am no parrot, but a man in my own place. Define a man. I walk upright. I think. I collate facts. I imagine. I anticipate. I learn. I speak.

What is a man by your definition?"

"Pretty Polly!" said the professors.

They were very angry. One of them hit the creature with his walking cane. No one likes to be set on a level with a beast. And the beast covered its face with its hands, and was silent.

It was warier when the mathematicians came. It added two and two together for them. They were amazed. It subtracted eight from ten. They wondered at it. It divided twenty by five. They marvelled. It took courage. It said:

"But you have reached a point where your formulae and calculuses fail. There is a simple law—one by which you reached the earth long ago—one by which you can leave it at will—"

The professors were furious.

"Parrot! Parrot!" they shouted.

"No! In my own place—"

The beast fell silent.

Then came the priests, smiling kindly—except to one another. For with each other they argued furiously and loathingly regarding their own views on rule and theory.

"Oh, stop!" said the creature, pleadingly.

It lifted it hands towards them and its golden eyes were full of pity.

"You make everything petty and meaningless," it said. "Let me tell you of the Master Plan of the universe. It is so simple and nothing to do with gods or rules, myths or superstition. Nothing to do with fear."

The priests were so outraged that they forgot to hate one another. They screamed wildly with one voice:

"Wicked!"

They fled from the creature, jamming in the cage door in their haste to escape and forget the soulless, evil thing. And the beast sighed and hid its sorrowful face, and took refuge in increasing silence.

The elders grew to hate it. They disliked the imitating and the parrot-talk, the golden eyes, the sorrow, the pity. They took away its chair, its table, its plate and cup. They ordered it to walk properly—on all fours, like any other beast.

"But in my own place—"

It broke off there. Yet some sort of pride, or stubbornness, or courage, made it refuse to crawl, no matter what they threatened or did.

They sold it to a circus.

A small sum was sent to the farmer who had first found the thing, and the rest of its price went into the state coffers for making weapons for a pending war.

The man who owned the circus was not especially brutal, as such men go. He was used to training beasts, for he was himself the chief attraction of the show, with his lions and tigers, half-drugged and toothless as they were. He said it was no use being too easy on animals.

"They don't understand over-kindness," said he. "They get to despising you. You have to show who's master."

He showed the creature who was master.

He made it jump through hoops and do simple sums on a blackboard. At first it also tried to speak to the people who came to look at it. It would say, in its soft and bell-clear tones:

"Oh, listen—I can tell you things—"

Everyone was amazed at its cleverness and most entertained by the eager way it spoke. And such parrot nonsense it talked!

"Hark at it!" they cried. "It wants to tell us things, bless it!"

"About the other side of the moon!"

"The far side of Saturn!"

"Who taught it to say all this stuff?"

"It's saying something about the block in mathematics now!"

"And the language of infinity!"

"Logic!"

"And the Master Plan!"

They rolled about, helpless with laughter in their ringside seats.

It was even more entertaining to watch the creature doing its sums on the big blackboard, which two attendants would turn so that everyone could admire the cleverness: 2 + 2, and the beautifully formed 4 that it wrote beneath. 10 – 8 = 2. 5 into 20—11 from 12.

"How clever it is," said a small girl, admiringly.

Her father smiled.

"It's the trainer who's clever," he said. "The animal knows nothing of what it does. Only what it has been taught. By kindness, of course," he added quickly, as the child looked sad.

"Oh, good," said she, brightening. "I wouldn't like it hurt. It's so sweet."

But even she had to laugh when it came to the hoop jumping. For the creature hated doing it. And, although the long whip of the trainer never actually touched its grey fur, yet it cowered at the cracking sound.

Surprising, if anyone had wondered why. And it ran, upright on its fine furred feet, and graceful in spite of the red and yellow clothes it was wearing, and it jumped through the hoops. And then more hoops were brought. And these were surrounded by inflammable material and set on fire. The audience was enthralled. For the beast was terrified of fire, for some reason. It would shrink back and clutch at its shoulder, its arm, its thigh. It would stare up wildly into the roof of the great circus canopy—as if it could see through it and out to the sky beyond—as though it sought desperately for help that would not come. And it shook and trembled. And the whip cracked. And it cried aloud as it came to each flaming hoop. But it jumped.

And it stopped talking to the people. Sometimes it would almost speak, but then it would give a hunted glance towards the ringmaster, and lapse into silence. Yet always it walked and ran and jumped as a man would do these things—upright. Not on all fours, like a proper beast.

And soon a particularly dangerous tightrope dance took the fancy of the people. The beast was sold to a small touring animal show. It was getting very poor in entertainment value, anyway. It moved sluggishly. Its fur was draggled and dull. It had even stopped screaming at the fiery hoops. And—it was such an eerie, manlike thing to have around. Everyone was glad to see it go.

In the dreary little show where it went, no one even pretended to understand animals. They just showed them in their cages. Their small, fetid cages. To begin with, the keeper would bring the strange creature out to perform for the onlookers. But it was a boring performance. Whip or no whip, hunger or less hunger, the beast could no longer run or jump properly. It shambled round and round, dull-eyed and silent. People merely wondered what sort of animal it was, but not with any great interest. It could hardly even be made to flinch at fire, not even when sparks touched its fur. It was sold to a collector of rare beasts. And he took it to his little menagerie on the edge of his estate near a forest.

He was not really very interested in his creatures. It was a passing hobby for a very rich man. Something to talk about among his friends. Only once he came to inspect his new acquisition. He prodded it with a stick. He thought it rather an ugly, dreary animal.

"I heard that you used to talk, parrot-fashion," said he. "Go on, then, say something."

It only cowered. He prodded it some more.

"I read about you when they had you in the city," said the man, prodding harder. "You used to talk, I know you did. So talk now. You used to say all sorts of clever things. That you were a man in your own place. Go on, tell me you're a man."

"Pretty Polly," mumbled the creature, almost inaudibly.

Nothing would make it speak again.

It was so boring that no one took much notice or care of it. And one night it escaped from its cage.

The last glimpse that anyone saw of it was by a hunter in the deeps of the forest.

It was going slowly looking in terror at rabbits and squirrels. It was weeping aloud and trying desperately to walk on all fours. ⚛

STUDY FOR CROUCHING NUDE
1952
Francis Bacon

From Science Fiction to Science Fact

JULIE NOBLES

Transplanted organs, rockets to the moon, the atom bomb, and cloning: believe it or not, all of these sprang to life in the pages of science fiction (SF) long before scientists turned them into reality.

The following SF writers have each put their own special stamp on the development of the genre, and each has made predictions about our future. Many of the old masters' wildly imaginative predictions are now reality. Only time will tell if the fiction of newer SF voices will also become fact.

MARY SHELLEY (1797-1851)

Shelley's famous novel, *Frankenstein*, written when she was just nineteen, is usually considered the first full-blown science fiction novel. It was written in installments to provide evening entertainment for guests at a country house where Shelley stayed.

KEY WORK: *Frankenstein*

FICTION TO FACT: electric shock to jumpstart the heart, transplanted organs, mechanical body parts

JULES VERNE (1828-1905)

Verne, a Frenchman, is known as.the founding father of modern science fiction. His popular novels emphasize the use of machines to tame and conquer the unknown.

KEY WORKS: *Journey to the Center of the Earth, From the Earth to the Moon, Twenty Thousand Leagues Under the Sea, Around the World in Eighty Days*

FICTION TO FACT: rockets to the moon, submarines, and in a little-known work *Paris in the 20th Century*, materialistic culture with overcrowded subways and fax machines

H.G. WELLS (1866-1946)

Considered a master by his contemporaries, Wells' influence on the SF tradition is immeasurable. He was the first SF author to actually be trained in the sciences and the first to write about alien invasions. His finely crafted novels combine criticism of contemporary society, speculation about the future, ingenious technology, and exotic adventure.

KEY WORKS: *The Time Machine, The War of the Worlds*

FICTION TO FACT: air warfare, the atom bomb, tanks, genetic engineering

ALDOUS HUXLEY (1894-1963)

Huxley's one great novel, *Brave New World*, suggests a future where technology, though used with good intentions by the government, nevertheless leads to a loss of both freedom and individualism.

KEY WORK: *Brave New World*

FICTION TO FACT: genetic engineering, cloning, virtual reality entertainment, drugs used for the relief of stress and anxiety

GEORGE ORWELL (1903-1950)

Unlike Huxley, who warned of the dangers of technology, Orwell wrote about political horrors – specifically totalitarian dictatorships. "Big Brother is watching you," "doublethink," and "newspeak" are words and phrases from *Nineteen Eighty-Four* that have become part of our language.

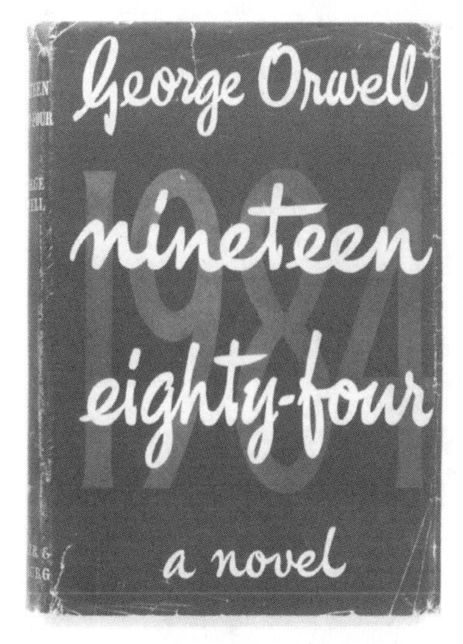

KEY WORKS: *Animal Farm, Nineteen Eighty-Four*

FICTION TO FACT: the crushing weight of dictatorships and the ensuing loss of freedoms, electronic spying, 'spin doctors' who turn and twist facts into pseudo-news

ROBERT HEINLEIN (1907-1988)

Many critics call Heinlein the most influential and innovative figure in American SF. He was the first to create a Future History, (an entire imaginary world and chronology) as the setting for many of his novels; he was the first to write SF specifically for younger audiences; and he almost single-handedly turned SF into a form that was accepted as 'literature' by literary critics. While his earlier works were lively and optimistic, his later writing became dark and highly controversial due to his increasingly right-wing notions about politics, gender, and the role of the military.

KEY WORKS: *Beyond This Horizon, Sixth Column, Double Star, Starship Troopers, Stranger in a Strange Land*

FICTION TO FACT? commercial exploitation of the moon, religious dictatorships, interstellar exploration, forced segregation of social 'misfits'

ISSAC ASIMOV (1920-1992)

Asimov, described as a 'workaholic geek,' authored more than 500 books during his lifetime. While many were SF novels and stories, a surprising number were nonfiction, ranging in subject matter from Shakespeare, to the Bible, to biochemistry, in which he had a Ph.D.

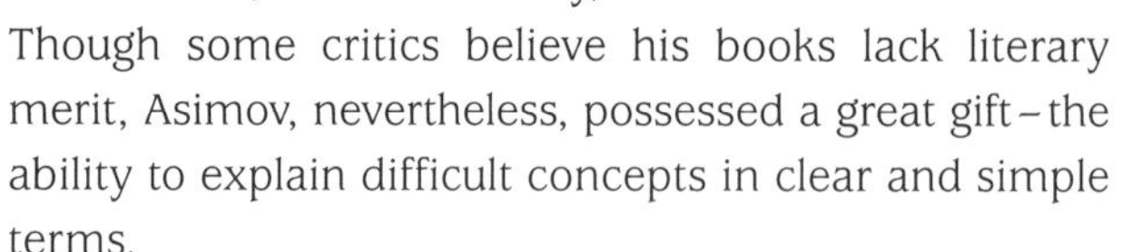

Though some critics believe his books lack literary merit, Asimov, nevertheless, possessed a great gift – the ability to explain difficult concepts in clear and simple terms.

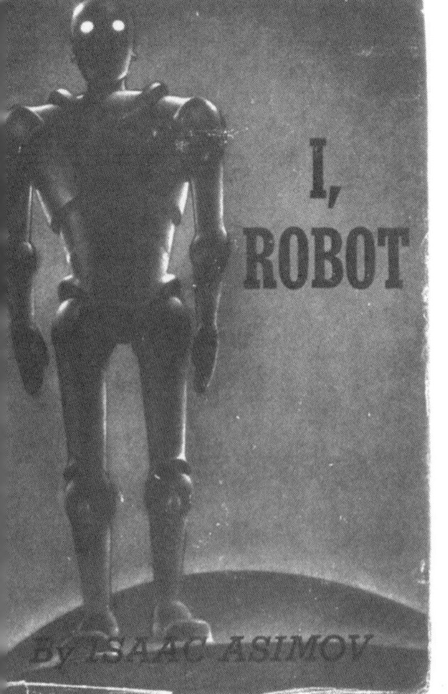

KEY WORKS: *I, Robot,* the *Foundation* trilogy, *The Gods Themselves*

FICTION TO FACT? robots in service to mankind, artificial intelligence, distance learning, harvesting energy from other universes

ARTHUR C. CLARKE (1917)

Arthur C. Clarke is a legend in the SF world. His name is forever linked to the novel *2001: A Space Odyssey* and the groundbreaking movie of the same name. In addition, Clarke's knowledge, sensitivity, and style made him an obvious choice as CBS' expert commentator for the Apollo moon missions.

KEY WORKS: *Against the Fall of Night, Childhood's End, 2001: A Space Odyssey, Rendevous with Rama, The Fountains of Paradise*

FICTION TO FACT? communication satellites, thinking computers, a 'space elevator' connecting earth with an end point in the galaxy, harvesting energy from sources on other planets, man's destruction of the earth

RAY BRADBURY (1920)

Although Bradbury is considered a SF master, his beautifully styled pieces are actually anti-science and anti-technology. While his characters travel to other worlds, the exotic settings are often secondary to the inner journeys of mind and spirit. In fact, much of his work looks backward rather than forward in a nostalgic quest for good times gone forever.

KEY WORKS: *Fahrenheit 451, Dandelion Wine, The Martian Chronicles*

FICTION TO FACT? earphones, transistor radios, TV as a replacement for reading, wall TV, colonization of other planets

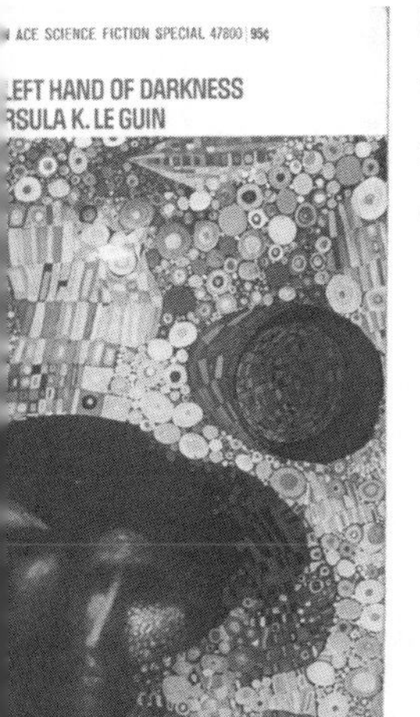

URSULA K. LE GUIN (1929)

Ursula K. Le Guin creates complex cultures on imaginary planets, yet serious themes such as gender roles and economic justice keep her stories down to earth.

KEY WORKS: *The Left Hand of Darkness,* the *Earthsea* series, *Always Coming Home*

FICTION TO FACT? alien visitors, telepathic communication, societal structure based on testing

Lose Now, Pay Later

CAROL FARLEY

I think my little brother is crazy. At least I hope he is. Because if his looney idea is right, then all of us are being used like a flock of sheep, and that's a pretty gruesome thought. Humans just can't be that stupid. My brother has a dumb idea, that's all. It's just a dumb idea.

This whole situation started about eight months ago. That's when I first knew anything about it, I mean. My best friend, Trinja, and I were shopping when we noticed a new store where an old insurance office used to be. It was a cubbyhole, really, at the far end of the mall where hardly anybody ever goes. We were there because we'd used that entrance as we came home from school.

"Swoodies!" Trinja said, pointing at the letters written across the display window. "What do think they are, Deb?"

I stared through the glass. The place had always looked dim and dingy before, full of desks, half-dead plants, and bored-looking people; but now it was as bright and glaring as a Health Brigade Corp office. There weren't any people inside at all, but there were five or six gold-colored machines lining the walls. Signs were hung everywhere.

SWEETS PLUS GOODIES = SWOODIES, one said. Flavors were posted by each machine; peanut-butter-fudge-crunch . . . butter-rum-pecan . . . chocolate-nut-mint . . . Things like that. The biggest sign of all simply said FREE.

I have to admit that the place gave me the creeps that first time I saw it. I don't know why. It just looked so bare and bright, so empty and clean, without any people or movement. The glare almost hurt my eyes. And I guess I was suspicious about anything that was completely free.

Still, though, there was a terrific aroma drifting out of there—sort of a combination of all those flavors that were listed on the signs.

"Let's go in," Trinja said, grabbing my arm. I could see that the smell was getting to her too. She's always on a diet, so she thinks about food a lot.

"But it's so empty in there," I said, drawing away.

"They've just opened, that's all," she told me, yanking my arm again. "Besides, machines and robots run lots of the stores. Let's go inside and see what's in there."

Do you know that wonderful spurt of air that rushes out when you first open an expensive box of candy? The inside of that store smelled just like the inside of one of those boxes. For a few seconds we just stood there sniffing and grinning. My salivary glands started swimming.

* * *

Trinja turned toward the nearest machine. "Coconut-almond-marshmallow." She was almost drooling. "I've got to try one, Deb." She pressed the button, and a chocolate cone dropped down, like a coffee cup from a kitcho machine. Then a mixture, similar to the look of soft ice cream, filled it. "Want to try it with me?" she asked, reaching for the cone. We both took a taste.

It was absolutely the neatest sensation I've had in my whole life. Swoodies aren't cold like ice cream or warm like cooked pudding, but they're a blending of both in temperature and texture. The flavor melts instantly, and your whole mouth and brain are flooded with tastes and impressions. Like that first swoodie I tried, coconut-almond-marshmallow; suddenly, as my mouth separated the individual tastes, my brain burst into memories associated with each flavor. I felt as if I were lying on a warm beach, all covered with coconut suntan oil—then I heard myself giggling and singing as a group of us roasted marshmallows around a campfire—then I relived the long-ago moments of biting into the special Christmas cookies my grandmother made with almonds when I was little.

"Wow!" Trinja looked at me, and I could see that she had just experienced the same kind of reactions. We scarfed up the rest of that swoodie in just a few more bites, and we moved on to another flavor. With each one it was the same. I felt a combination of marvelous tastes and joyous thoughts. We tried every flavor before we finally staggered out into the mall again.

"I'll have to diet for a whole year now," Trinja said, patting her stomach.

"I feel like a blimp myself," I told her, but neither one of us cared. We both felt terrific. "Go ahead in there," I called to some grade-school kids who were looking at the store. "You'll love those swoodies."

"It's a publicity stunt, we think," Trinja told them. "Everything is free in there."

In no time at all the news about the swoodie shop had spread all over town. But days passed, and still everything was absolutely free. Nobody knew who the new owners were or why they were giving away their product. Nobody cared. The mall directors said a check arrived to pay for the rent, and that was all they were concerned about. The Health Brigade Corp said swoodies were absolutely safe for human consumption.

Swoodies were still being offered free a month later, but the shop owners had still not appeared. By then nobody cared. There were always long lines of people in front of the place, but the swoodies tasted so good nobody minded waiting for them. And the supply was endless. Soon more shops like the first one began opening in other places around the city, with machines running in the same quiet, efficient way. And everything was still absolutely free.

Soon all of us were gaining weight like crazy.

"It's those darn swoodies," Trinja told me as we left the mall after our daily binge. "I can't leave them alone. Each one must have a thousand calories, but I still pig out on them."

I sighed as I walked out into the sunshine. "Me too. If only there was some easy way to eat all the swoodies we want and still not gain any weight!"

* * *

The words were hardly out of my mouth when I noticed a new feature in the mall parking lot. Among all the usual heliobiles there was a tall white plastic box, sort of like those big telephone booths you see in old pictures. A flashing sign near the booth said THE SLIMMER. A short, thin woman was standing beside it. She was deeply tanned, and her head was covered with a green turban almost the same color as the jumpsuit she was wearing.

Trinja looked at the sign, then glanced at the woman. "What's that mean?"

"It means that this machine can make you slimmer," the woman answered. She had a deep, strange-sounding voice. "Just step inside, and you'll lose unwanted fat."

She seemed so serious and confident that I was startled. In the old days people thought they could lose weight in a hurry, but those of us who live in 2041 aren't that gullible. No pills or packs or wraps or special twenty-four-hour diets can work. There isn't any easy way to get rid of fat, and that's all there is to it. I knew this booth was a scam or a joke of some kind, but the woman acted as if it were a perfectly respectable thing. Her seriousness sort of unnerved me. I looked into the booth half expecting someone to jump out laughing. But it was empty, stark white, and, except for some overhead grill work, it was completely smooth and bare.

"How can a thing like this make you slimmer?" I asked.

The woman shrugged. "A new process. Do you care to try? Twenty-five yen to lose one pound of body fat."

Trinja and I both burst into laughter. "And how long is it before the pound disappears?" she asked.

The woman never even cracked a smile. "Instantly. Body fat is gone instantly." She gestured to a small lever on the side nearest to her. "I regulate the power flow according to your payment."

★ ★ ★

My mouth dropped open. "But that's impossible! No exercise? No chemicals? No starving on a retreat week?"

"No." The woman folded her arms and leaned against the smooth white sides of her cubicle, as if she didn't much care whether we tried her new process or not. Trinja and I stared at each other. I was wondering if the woman had tried her machine herself—she didn't have an ounce of fat.

"You got any money?" I asked Trinja. As she was shaking her head, I was rummaging through my pack. "I've got a hundred and thirty yen."

"Five pounds then," the woman said, taking my money with one hand and setting her lever with the other. She literally pushed me into the booth, and the door slammed behind me.

At first I wanted to scream because I was so scared. The whole thing had happened too fast. I wanted to prove that this woman and her slimmer were a big joke, but suddenly I was trapped in a coffinlike structure as bare and as bright as an old microwave oven. My heart was hammering, and the hair on the back of my neck stood up straight. I opened my mouth, but before I could scream, there was a loud humming sound, and instantly the door flew open again. I saw Trinja's frightened face peering in at me.

"Are you all right, Deb? Are you okay? I guess she decided not to do anything after all. You ought to get your money back."

"Five pounds are gone," the woman said in her strange voice.

Trinja pulled me away. "I'll just bet!" she shouted back at the woman. "Somebody ought to report you and that phony machine! We might even call the Health Brigade Corp!" She leaned closer to me. "Are you really okay, Deb?"

I took a deep breath. "My jeans feel loose."

Frowning, Trinja shook her head. "It's just your imagination, that's all. What a fake! I think that woman was wacko, Debbie, really weird. The only thing slimmer after a treatment like that is your bank account. Nobody but nobody can lose weight that easily. We'll go to my house, and you can weigh yourself. You haven't lost an ounce."

But Trinja was wrong. I really *was* five pounds lighter. I know it sounds impossible, but Trinja's calshow is never wrong. The two of us hopped and howled with joy. Then we ravaged her bedroom trying to find some more money. We ran all the way back to the mall, worrying all the way

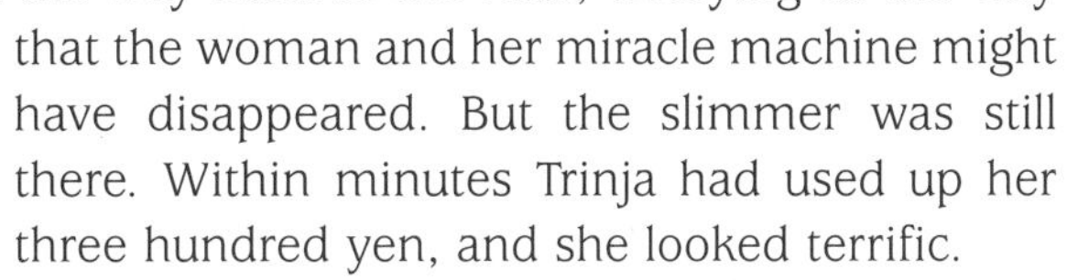

that the woman and her miracle machine might have disappeared. But the slimmer was still there. Within minutes Trinja had used up her three hundred yen, and she looked terrific.

"I can't believe it! I just can't believe it!" she kept saying as she notched her belt tighter. "Twelve pounds gone in seconds!"

"For safety's sake I'll have to prick your wrist, my dear," the woman said. "For every ten pounds you lose we give a tiny little mark. Nobody will ever notice it."

"It didn't even hurt," Trinja said as we walked home. And neither of us could see the tiny blue pinprick unless we looked closely. We were both so happy about the weight loss that we almost floated. All our worries and problems about calories and fat and diets were over forever.

In no time at all the slimmers were all over the city, near all the swoodie stores. They've been a real blessing. Everybody says so. Now there's hardly a fat person left on the streets. A few people have so many blue marks on their wrists that you can see them, but most have just four or five pinpricks.

Nobody really understands how these slimmers work. The attendants, all just as strange sounding as the woman in our mall, get so technical in their explanations that none of us can follow the principles they're talking about, so we don't much worry about it. The process has something to do with invisible waves that can change fat cells into energy, which then radiates away from the body.

"I don't care how the slimmers work," Trinja says happily. "Now I can eat swoodies all day long if I want, and I never gain an ounce. That's all I care about."

Everybody feels that way, I guess. We're too happy to want to upset anything by asking questions. Maybe that's why you don't hear about the swoodies or slimmers on the fax or the bodivision or read about them anywhere. Nobody understands them well enough to sound very intelligent about them. But people all over Earth are beginning to use them. My cousin in Tokyo faxed to say that they have them in her area now and people there are just as happy as we are.

Except for my brother, Trevor. He's not the least bit happy, he says. Of course, few ten-year-olds worry about weight, so he doesn't know the joy of being able to eat everything in sight and still stay thin.

"Suppose the swoodies and the slimmers are run by aliens from outer space," he says. "From lots farther than we've been able to go. Maybe they have big starships posted around Earth, and they're gathering up the energy from human fat that's sent up from the slimmers. Maybe the swoodies are here so people will get fat quicker so that there'll be more to harvest through the slimmer machines. Then they'll take the fat back to their planet and use it as fuel."

"That's the dumbest thing I ever heard of!" Trinja has told him. "Why don't we hear about the spaceships, then? Why doesn't the Health Brigade Corp tell us to stop doing this if it isn't good for us?"

* * *

Trevor thinks he has the answers. He says the spaceships are invisible to human detection, and he says the aliens have hypnotized our leaders into being as calm and placid as we all are. The blue marks on our wrists play a big role. He says maybe after each of us has had so many blue marks, we'll be culled from the flock because our fat content won't be as good anymore.

He's crazy, isn't he? He must think we all have the brains of sheep. Ten-year-old brothers can be a real pain. He simply doesn't know people yet, that's all. Humans would never sacrifice their freedom and dignity just so they could eat and still be thin. Even aliens ought to know that.

I could quit eating swoodies and using those slimmers any time I want to.

But all those little blue marks Trinja and I have are beginning to look like delicate tattooed bracelets, and we both think they look really neat on our wrists.

The Water Traders' Dream

ROBERT PRIEST

All the water traders
who trade in outer space
talk of a distant planet—
a magical, mystical place
that has seas and seas full of water,
sweet water beyond all worth.
They say that planet is green in the sun
and the name of that planet is Earth.

And the people there drink the water,
they dive and swim in it too.
It falls from the sky in water storms
and it comes in the morning as dew.
That sweet, sweet water is everywhere—
Sweet water! Sweet water of Earth!
And the traders say that the people there
have no idea what it's worth.

So the traders have their earth dreams.
They dream of one silver cup
brought back across space from the earthlings
for millions to drink it up.
'Sweet water! Sweet water! Sweet water of Earth!
The people there trade it for gold!
They've no idea what water's worth—
just look how much they've sold!'

They dream the dream of a water storm
surely it would drive one mad
to have a wind-full of water flung in your face,
to sail in it like Sinbad!
Yes, they say there are whole oceans there
where waves break on the shore,
where winds leave water singing
and the sunlight makes it roar!

They say that those who live there
just don't know its true worth.
They say that planet is green in the sun
and the people there call it the Earth.

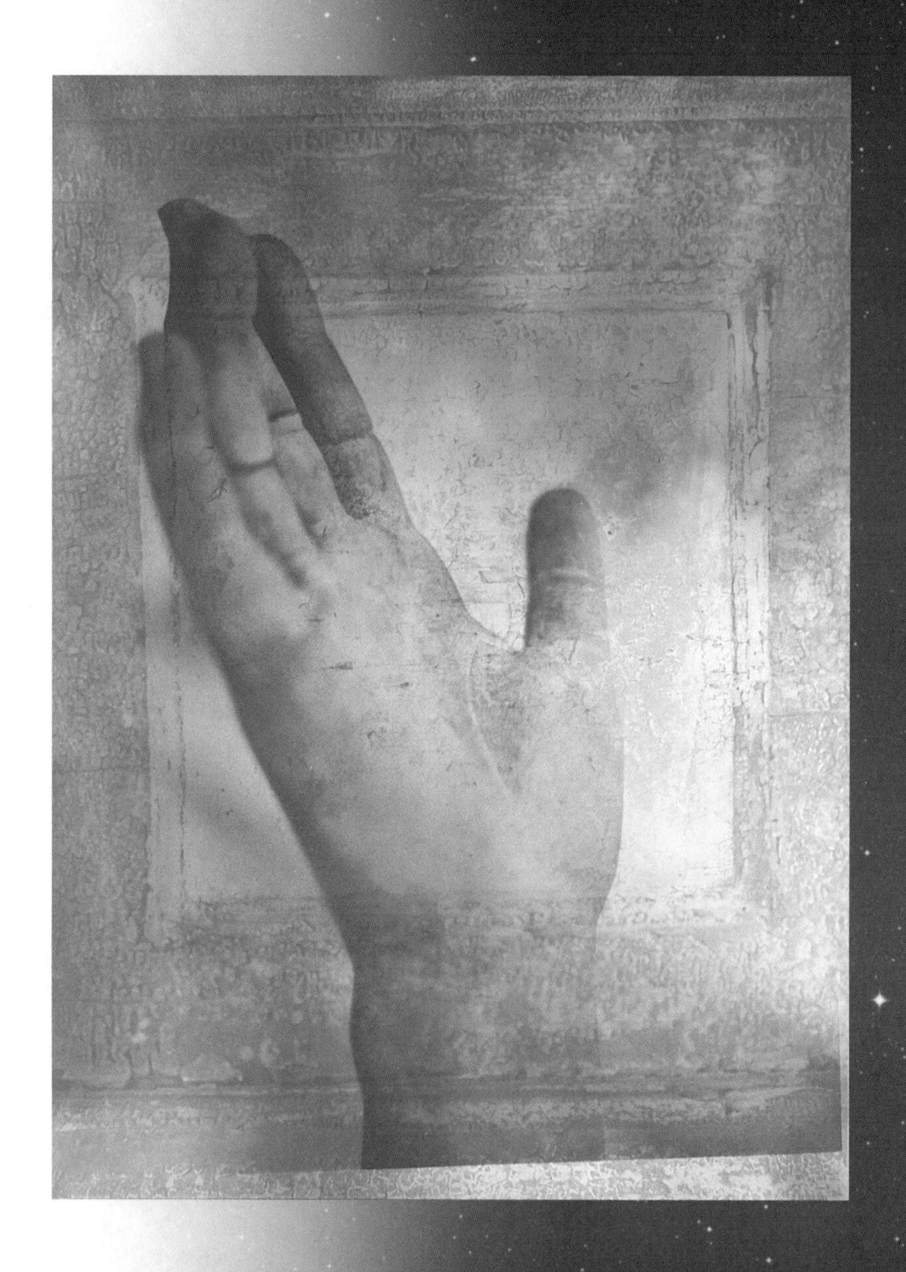

The Helping Hand

NORMAN SPINRAD

FIRST CONTACT WITH EXTRATERRESTRIAL CIVILIZATION

HOUSTON. NASA has confirmed that the anomalous radio pulses emanating from Barnard's star that NASA SETI[1] researchers discovered nearly a month ago are definitely artificial.

"We haven't decoded the signals yet, but they clearly are data packets," Dr. Henry Brancusi, head of the NASA team, declared. "They repeat every 33 hours. Most peculiar. As the closest candidate for a star with a habitable zone, Barnard's was one of the earliest targets of the first SETI researchers, but nothing had ever been detected before. It's as if they've just gone on the air."

—*Science News*

SPACE TELESCOPE DETECTS INHABITED PLANET

LUNAGRAD. The Greater European Space Agency has confirmed the existence of a technological civilization on the fourth planet of Barnard's star. The GESA massive optical array on the far side of the moon has detected a ring of satellite-sized objects in perfect Geosychronous orbit around the planet.

"It can't be anything else," said Leonid Vyshinkov, director of the MOA station. "We are looking at a high technical civilization. There is no further reason to doubt that we are indeed receiving a message from intelligent beings on the fourth planet of Barnard's star."

—*L'Espresso*

1 **SETI:** acronym that stands for the Search for Extraterrestrial Intelligence

INTERSTELLAR PRIME TIME?

NEW HOLLYWOOD. Jack Kovacs, head of Universal-Toho-Disney Productions, announced today that UTDP technicians had succeeded in decoding the transmissions from Barnard's star.

"It's television, what else?" Kovacs told reporters. "Scientists may have been trying to get fancy equations out of it, but I knew that couldn't be the bottom line, I mean, if we were transmitting to them, wouldn't we send something with real production values? The broadcast quality isn't exactly professional, but we're bringing it up to industry standards in the processing lab, and we're going to release it on November 12."

—Variety

SECRETARY GENERAL DEMANDS FREE RELEASE OF BARNARD TRANSMISSION

NEW YORK. United Nations Secretary General Wolfgang Steinholtz demanded today that Universal-Toho-Disney Productions release the television transmission from the Barnards that they claim to have decoded through the auspices of the United Nations International Press Agency, rather than selling commercial rights to the program for outrageous prices as planned.

"It's perfectly disgusting to engage in such profiteering with the greatest event in human history," he declared. "This message was meant for all mankind. The Barnards certainly could never have intended that their transmission become the property of a television studio."

"This Secretary General guy's got to be coming from outer space himself," said Jack Kovacs, President of UTDP, when reached for comment in New Hollywood. "What does he expect us to do, give away the biggest world audience share in history? The rights to this are gonna be worth at least a billion and a half dollars!"

Kovacs went on to express indignation at the public outcry. "It's not as if we were ripping off the Barnards or something," he insisted. "We're setting up an escrow account for them even though we don't have to. And we're giving them 17 percent of the producer's net profit. Even major stars don't get a sweet deal like that. Does *that* sound like we're a bunch of sleazebag schlockmeisters?"

—The New York Times

OPENING CREDITS

FIRST CONTACT

A Universal-Toho-Disney Production
Produced in conjunction with the people of Barnard's star

FADE IN

A planet floating in space, fleecy cloud-cover over blue seas, green-and-brown continents, looking very much like another Earth, but with different continental outlines, less water, more land.

A series of helicopter shots. Thick jungles of fluffy green trees like enormous dustmops. Rolling savannas covered with lumpy yellowish moss. Seacoast swamps, where tangles of vines drip from huge bushes rooted in the mud. Mountain meadows dotted with clusters of round blue cacti. An enormous canyon with a lucent blue river at the bottom and waves of vegetation foaming down its soft ancient slopes.

Another series of shots, these of wildlife in medium close-up. A large six-legged purple herbivore cropping moss. A bright yellow bird with two pairs of wings. A monstrous blue-and-red striped upright biped[2] with four brawny arms ending in clusters of razor-sharp claws. A silvery torpedo-shape with six great fins, leaping and whirling out of the surface of the sea.

Cut to a full shot of two upright creatures standing hand-in-hand-in-hand-in-hand. Two pairs of arms, one pair of legs, round roly-poly bodies like teddy bears. One wears a bright blue togalike[3] affair, the other a white suit with an extra set of long, belled sleeves, and a short black cloak. What is visible of their skin is covered with short, lustrous, golden fur.

2 **biped:** a two-footed animal

3 **togalike:** like a toga, a loose, draped gown worn in public by citizens of ancient Rome

They have ovoid heads with large membranous ears, like the wings of golden bats. They have faces. Two large eyes with thin red sclera[4] and large black pupils, set too close together under bushy red brows. Big round light-purple lips that iris open and shut continually as if blowing fat wet kisses. No nose, but a mobile tubular projection covered with black fur depending from their stubby chins like elephants' trunks.

They look quite alien.

Alien, but cute.

They look into the camera, they touch the tips of their trunks together, they stretch them out toward the viewer as if in greeting.

A tracking shot on a small group of the same creatures, naked now, loping across a savanna, carrying rocks and short sharpened sticks. Some have single mounds on their chests, others bulbous yellow protuberances high up on their torsos.

Dissolve to another tribe of Barnards harvesting a field of blue-headed grain in whirlwind four-handed style, using short stone scythes.[5] Dissolve to a village of mud huts. Dissolve to a town of low brown stone buildings all crowded in against each other. Dissolve to a great warren of wood-and-plaster buildings piled high up against a cliff. Dissolve to a great freestanding metal and concrete city in the same style. Dissolve to a fleet of trimaran[6] barges lumbering through heavy seas under round balloon sails. Dissolve to a four-winged aircraft like an ungainly ornithopter, piloted by a Barnard in a tight black flight suit. Dissolve to an aerial shot of a complex highway system, with thousands of round six-wheeled cars careening around it at breakneck speed.

A rapidly cut tour montage of the wonders of Barnard civilization. Great gleaming cities. Endless fields of straight-rowed crops. Huge floating platforms clogging the surface of the sea. Strange machinelike factories puffing out clouds of thick brown smoke. Ungainly-looking squat rockets blasting off the pad. The planet seen through the porthole of some sort of space vehicle.

4 **sclera:** the white part of the eyeball

5 **scythes:** implements used for mowing or harvesting grain

6 **trimaran:** sailboats with three hulls side by side

Two naked Barnards pummeling each other with four pairs of fists. Two squads of Barnards in leather armor slicing each other to bits with short recurved hand-swords. Two armies of Barnards laying each other waste with guns. A village set ablaze by the napalm projectors of big round tanks crunching through it on six enormous bladed wheels. A fleet of ominous black warplanes circling a burning city like angry dragonflies. A roiling, boiling mushroom-pillar cloud.

A series of slow dissolves revealing endless variations on rubble and ruin. Burned-out skeletons of buildings. Vast vistas of charred fields where nothing lives. Huge smoking craters. Frozen lakes of fused black glass. Forests burning. Rivers churning with debris.

Dead birds falling out of a poisonous brown sky. A shoreline choked with the rotting carcasses of sea animals. Decaying jungles of dead vegetation. Mobs of refugees, their golden fur gone all mangy and falling out in patches to reveal angry pink skin, fleeing a series of dead cities under ominous black-and-brown thunderheads.

Darkness. Sheets of dirty gray rain. Howling blizzards. Great glaciers creeping out of their mountain strongholds and onto the plain in time-lapse majesty. Snowdrifts piling up to hide the corpses of cities, jungles, savannas, shoreline marshes, animals, Barnards, a whole formerly living world.

Cut to the opening shot, the fourth planet of Barnard's star, verdant and vital, as it floats in the blackness of space, looking very much like a second Earth.

The fleecy white cloud cover slowly turns an ugly chemical brown that diffuses out to enrobe the planet in a mist of foul choking smog. Brilliant balls of light explode on the surface, one, two, three, then dozens, scores, hundreds, as dark black fountains pour radioactive soot into the atmosphere. Whole swatches of continents are set ablaze. The atmosphere darkens, turns a uniform gray, begins to blacken.

Then it suddenly clears as if the special-effects department has just turned off the smoke machine, and we see the planet below with a sudden new clarity. Continents gleam a skeletal white. Great icebergs drift in the equatorial[7] seas. Jagged ranges of cold gray mountaintops peak up out of the endless ice sheets.

A series of low helicopter shots. Nothing but snowdrifts and ice sheets at first, but then, here and there, huge metal domes dug like enormous igloos into the snow, few, and scattered, and pathetic in all that dead white immensity.

A series of quickly cut shots of the interiors of the domes, grim corridors full of mangy, diseased-looking Barnards, huge chemical vats, Barnards eating what looks like slices of gray plastic, a family of Barnards crowded into a tiny steel-colored cubicle, Barnards unmistakably defecating into the recycling vats.

Cut to two Barnards standing hand-in-hand-in-hand-in-hand, staring at the camera, their fur falling out now, ugly sores along their trunks, their eyes watery with rheum.[8]

Slowly, without taking their eyes off the camera, they let go of each other's hands, get down on their knees, hang their heads in an unmistakable gesture of shame.

Then they hold all their arms out before them, turn up their fleshy palms as if to catch something falling from the heavens. Slowly they raise their gaze skyward, and lift up their trunks imploringly, like elephants reaching for the peanut held by a small child just beyond their grasp.

The camera follows the line of their eyes, the line of their trunks, upward, into a brilliant starry night. The angle reverses, and now we are looking down at two lorn golden creatures kneeling on an endless sheet of ice, gazing up longingly out of the desolation at us, their scabrous trunks reaching out desperately for whatever we have to give.

FADE TO BLACK

7 **equatorial:** located at the equator

8 **rheum:** watery discharge

A GRIM WARNING

MOSCOW. The opinion in the world scientific community is all but unanimous. The Barnard civilization followed an evolution quite similar to our own until they reached the point where we are now, with industrial pollution at the point of poisoning the atmosphere and killing off the biosphere, and nuclear weapons proliferating beyond control. Then they had a nuclear war which altered their planet's albedo[9] and brought on a Nuclear Winter and what appears to be a permanent worldwide ice age.

We have been shown the future we are making. If we do not cease polluting our atmosphere, we *will* destroy its ability to support a biosphere. If we stumble into nuclear war, we *will* bring on a Nuclear Winter.

The message that the few pathetic survivors of the Barnard catastrophe have sent us is all too clear—we must mend our ways or die.

—Pravda

POPE CHIDES WORLD SELFISHNESS

VATICAN CITY. The Holy Father today chastised the world for its selfish response to the tragic message from Barnard's star. "To take this message as merely a warning sent for our own benefit betrays a lack of Christian charity," John XXV declared. "It is clearly a desperate plea for help. And if we fail to hold out a helping hand, we will have proven ourselves unworthy of survival. We must do whatever we can to aid our suffering fellow creatures on the fourth planet of Barnard's star."

—L'Osservatore Romano

BRAZIL BANS ALL AMAZON EXPLOITATION

RIO DE JANEIRO. President Antonio Da Silva today issued an emergency edict banning all further burning, logging, mining, clear-cutting, and industrial activity in the entire Amazon basin. "This will require great economic sacrifices on the part of the Brazilian people," he said, "but we now know that we have no choice. The trees of our great national patrimony[10] provide the air that *we* breathe too."

—Jornal do Brasil

9 **albedo:** ability to reflect light
10 **patrimony:** inheritance

NUCLEAR WINTER REVERSIBLE?

LONDON. "The effects of nuclear winter can be reversed," Dr. Gareth Wilson suggested today. "Finely divided carbon dusted on the ice sheets would increase absorption of sunlight and melt them over time. Once enough ice is melted, albedo will be decreased to the point where the melting process will become self-sustaining."

—Science

FRANCE JOINS BRITAIN IN DESTROYING NUCLEAR WEAPONS

—Le Monde

NEW LIFE FOR THE BARNARDS?

PALO ALTO. Genentech scientists have formulated a plan to reseed the fourth planet of Barnard's star with a viable new biosphere from Earth. Terrestrial organisms could be transported as germ plasm, re-engineered on the spot to adapt to local conditions, cloned using existing techniques, and then spread by conventional means. Reviving the entire planet might take centuries, but once the processes were started, life could be counted upon to spread itself into every available open ecological niche.

—Time

ISRAEL JOINS FORMER NUCLEAR CLUB

—Jerusalem Post

RED CROSS ANNOUNCES BARNARD RELIEF FUND

GENEVA. The International Red Cross has established a fund to raise the money needed to mount a relief mission to Barnard's star. Donations will be accepted from governments, corporations, and individual contributors.

—UPI

IT CAN BE DONE, NASA DECLARES

HOUSTON. NASA officials admitted today that it would be technologically possible to send a relief expedition to Barnard's star. A large spaceship could reach Barnard's star within a century using an interstellar ram-scoop drive already on the theoretical drawing boards, though it would push human technology to its limits.

The cost, however, is estimated at at least one trillion dollars.

—Houston Post

DENMARK PASSES BARNARD TAX

COPENHAGEN. The Danish parliament has voted approval of a 5 percent blanket sales tax with the receipts to be turned over to the Barnard Relief Fund. "If it can be done, it must be done," King Victor declared afterward. "We are a small country, but someone must be prepared to show the way."

—TASS

THE NETHERLANDS, ITALY, NEW ZEALAND, MALAWI ADOPT BARNARD TAX

UNITED STATES COMMITS LONG-TERM MATCHING FUNDS

WASHINGTON. President Wolfowitz has signed into law a bill to reduce the Defense budget by 10 percent a year for the next ten years and deposit the savings on a matching basis in the Barnard Relief Fund. The United States has committed itself by this action to financing 17 percent of the Barnard rescue mission.

—CNN

SOVIET UNION ANNOUNCES NUCLEAR DISARMAMENT

MOSCOW. President Gorchenko announced today that the Soviet Union would cease the manufacture of all nuclear weapons and destroy those it now possesses on a unilateral basis. "To use them, even in self-defense, would mean the death of our entire planet," he pointed out. "We are all dependent on the goodwill of each other for survival. The Barnards have shown us that that has always been true.”

Following the example set by the United States, the money formerly devoted to the production and maintenance of the nuclear deterrent will be deposited in the Barnard Relief Fund.

—Izvestia

THE *HELPING HAND* IS ON ITS WAY!

FROM ORBIT. The starship *Helping Hand* has at last begun its long voyage, carrying an international crew of two hundred, carbon extraction equipment, and frozen germ plasm for a new biosphere to the fourth planet of Barnard's star.

Just as the billions of people who contributed what they could to make this moment possible will never live to see the results, neither will the original crew of the *Helping Hand*. But when their sons and daughters arrive, our sons and daughters will remember that when their ancestors were called upon, we rose to the occasion and did what had to be done.

Today we have proven that the Barnards were not wrong to pin their last hope on the peoples of the Earth.

Or rather, perhaps, today we have at last become a people worthy of that choice.

—The New York Times

REPORT TO EARTH #337

The fourth planet of Barnard's star is an airless cold rock that never held life. There is nothing at all in orbit around it. Our scientists have not discovered so much as organic precursors.

The trillions of dollars contributed to this relief mission by the peoples of the Earth at enormous sacrifice to themselves, the best efforts of a generation of scientists, the entire lives of our mothers and fathers, have all been for naught. We have spent all our own lives in this cramped starship, and we will never live to see the Earth we have never known.

All for nothing.

We have all been victimized by the cruelest hoax in history.

But why? And how? And by whom?

—EDUARDO JONES

CAPTAIN, THE *Helping Hand*

REPORT TO EARTH #338

Oh my God, it's enormous! It just appeared out of nowhere, and now it's in a matching orbit with us and closing fast, a shimmering globe the size of a small moon! It's not only impossible to describe, my eyes don't seem to be able to form a clear image of it, there's a glow, and things like machinery in constant motion inside, and . . . and the ship is being drawn toward it!

The engines won't respond!

There's . . . there's some kind of opening that just appeared on the surface . . . a hole . . . a tunnel. . . .

We're being pulled inside! It's filled with light, it almost seems alive, it—

—EDUARDO JONES

CAPTAIN, THE *Helping Hand*

REPORT TO EARTH #339

We are children at the feet of the gods, primitive savages who have unwittingly sailed our little canoe into the harbor of a mighty celestial city. And yet, so they have told us, we have become something much more.

The *Helping Hand* was drawn down a long semitranslucent tunnel, through what seemed like some kind of city or machine or organism, towering structures of metal and glass and light that seemed almost organic in their constant flowing motion, and then the ship came to rest, gently suspended about a meter above the floor of a space so enormous that the ceiling disappeared into a shimmering mirage.

It may sound foolish in this report, but you had to be there to understand. We *had* to all meet this moment together, as the representatives of our species, as the family of man. Nothing else would have been right.

And so I led the entire crew out of the ship, to stand there, dazzled and blinking, in the center of a vast amphitheater.

Tiered high all around us, suspended by immaterial forces, were thousands upon thousands of creatures I cannot even begin to describe. Creatures of flesh and creatures of metal and creatures that appeared to be mobile plants. Creatures so beautiful they brought joy to the spirit and creatures so hideous that they made the skin crawl. Hundreds of different species, thousands perhaps, like a vast United Nations General Assembly of the stars.

The sound that they were making together was thunderous. There were clicks, and groans, and whinings, and buzzes, and whistles, and clackings, but the total effect was unmistakable, and it raised the hair on the back of the neck, and brought tears to the eyes.

It was applause.

Then a huge but somehow intimate voice spoke to us. It spoke to each of us in our own native tongue. It spoke with all the languages of the Earth with the collective voice of all those myriad creatures.

"Welcome, brothers," it said. "Welcome, people of the Earth," it said. "You have proven yourselves worthy. We greet you with joy."

"Worthy?" I stammered. "Worthy of what?"

"Worthy of joining the Interstellar Brotherhood of Sentient Beings. Worthy of joining those who have passed the test."

"Test? What test?" I demanded, outrage overcoming all sense of awe, for of course I knew the answer even as I shouted the question.

And of course I was right.

Yes, this galaxy-spanning civilization had created the Barnards out of whole cloth, created the false images and the completely fabricated plea for help on the part of a dying people who had never existed.

And of course I demanded of these cruel tricksters what you no doubt are demanding now as you hear this.

"How dare you do such a thing?" I cried in a fearless rage. "Billions of people sacrificed to make this mission possible! Our own planet was half dead itself when we received your lying message, it stretched us to our limits and beyond! Our parents willingly gave their whole lives to save your fictitious Barnards! And so have we! How dare you call us brothers after what you've done?"

"All of us have been tested. All of us have been forced to face the best that was in our hearts. And so all of us are brothers in the same true spirit. Surely in moving you to join us we have done you no harm."

"No harm!"

"Have you not put war behind you? Have you not learned to cross the gulfs between the stars and come unto *us*? And in the process of seeking to bring new life to the people of a dying planet become the true stewards of your own? And become the best that was in you? Is this not the greatest of gifts? And all the greater for being one you were allowed to give to *yourselves*?"

We all fell silent. For it was true. It was a cruel gift but a great one. It was ruthless and loving. It was very wise.

"So now we welcome you to the Interstellar Brotherhood of Sentient Beings, people of the Earth. We welcome you as equals in the deepest and truest sense. As a people who have earned the right to join us."

"Earned what?" someone muttered aloud. "What are you really offering us?"

There was a sound, a gesture, a feeling, that passed across all those faces, mouths, arms, tentacles, visages, of all those assembled creatures, a sound, a gesture, an emotional expression, and if it indeed was a kind of laughter, it was a laughter that made us all proud.

"Only what you yourselves offered to the Barnards," declared the voice of the Brotherhood. "Only that which makes us all brothers of the same sentient spirit. The best that we have at the full stretch of our powers, and perhaps a little beyond. What else do any of us have to offer but an open heart and a helping hand?"

And so now our little canoe begins the long voyage home across the stellar sea, refitted with engines that will take us there in our lifetimes, bearing the vast treasures of knowledge from the celestial city that we have found.

But the greatest treasure we bear home is the one we brought with us. The most precious knowledge we carry is what we knew all along.

—EDUARDO JONES

CAPTAIN, THE *Helping Hand*

Responding to Cluster Three

What Can We Learn From Science Fiction?

Thinking Skill DRAWING CONCLUSIONS

1. Consider the story "Puppet Show" from the last cluster and "Star Beast" from this cluster. Draw some **conclusions** about the main message of each story. Are the messages the same or do they differ? Explain your response.
2. Why do you think humans refuse to credit the Star Beast with intelligence and feelings?
3. In "Lose Now, Pay Later," the narrator says that "humans would never sacrifice their freedom and dignity just so they could eat and still be thin." Do you agree? Why or why not.
4. One way poets can convey meaning is through the placement of their words on the page. What is unusual about the form of "The Water Traders' Dream"? What do you think this form adds to the meaning of the poem?
5. Do you think earth's people could ever join together to solve a problem as they did in "The Helping Hand"? If yes, list some circumstances that might cause unified action; if no, explain your reasons.

Writing Activity: Life's Little Lessons

Review the three short stories and one poem in this cluster and **draw conclusions** about the lessons that could be learned from each selection. Restate each lesson as a moral. Examples of morals are:

Don't Count Your Chickens Before They Are Hatched

A Bird in the Hand Is Worth Two in the Bush

Don't Bite the Hand That Feeds You

Slow and Steady Wins the Race

A Well-Stated Moral

- uses clear, concise word choice
- expresses the idea of a teaching or lesson in just a few words
- often makes use of figurative language to explain abstract concepts (For example the moral that begins, "A Bird in the Hand . . ." is not really about birds, but about greed and wisdom.)

CLUSTER FOUR

THINKING ON YOUR OWN

Thinking Skill SYNTHESIZING

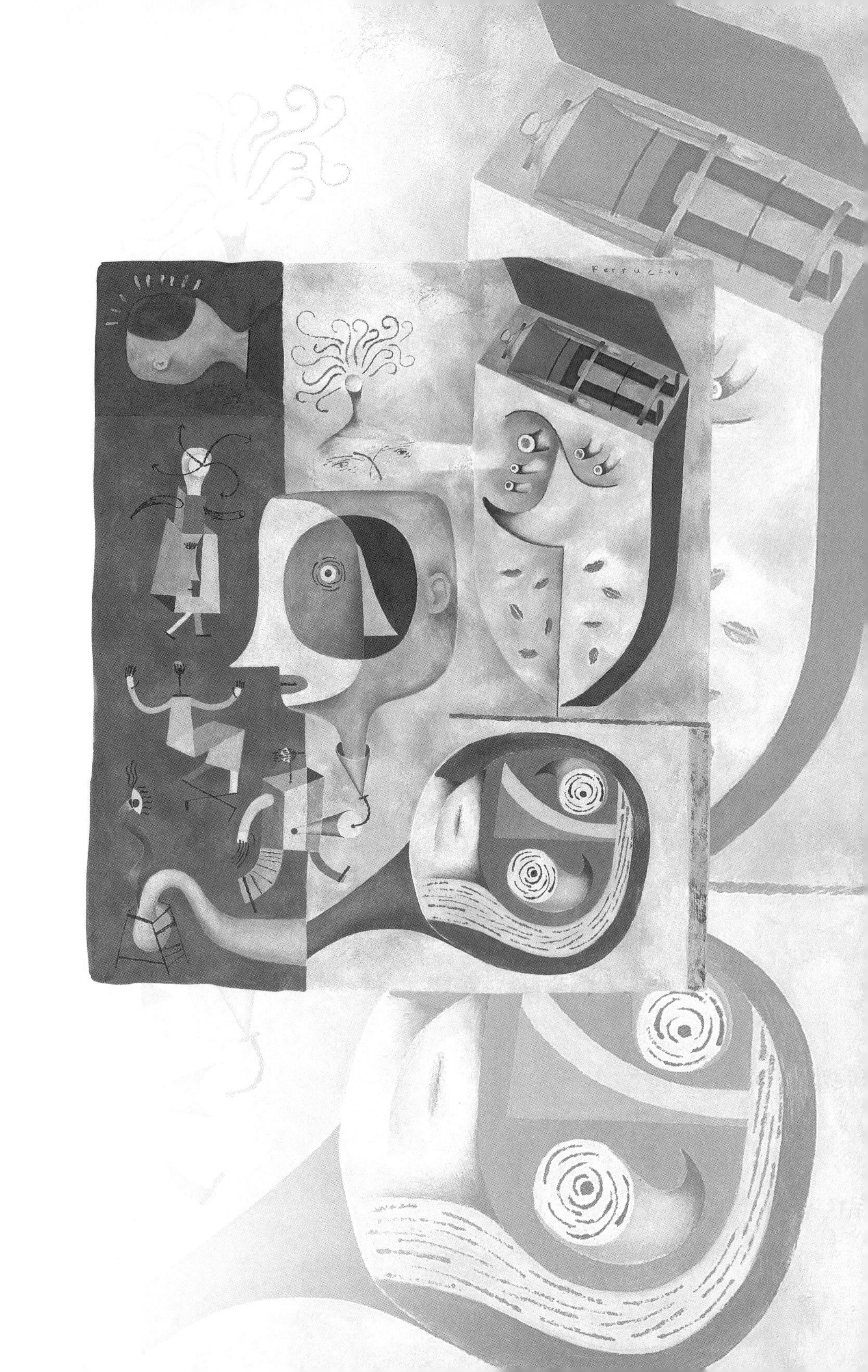

SQ

Ursula K. Le Guin

I think what Dr. Speakie has done is wonderful. He is a wonderful man. I believe that. I believe that people need beliefs. If I didn't have my belief I really don't know what would happen.

And if Dr. Speakie hadn't truly believed in his work he couldn't possibly have done what he did. Where would he have found the courage? What he did proves his genuine sincerity.

There was a time when a lot of people tried to cast doubts on him. They said he was seeking power. That was never true. From the very beginning all he wanted was to help people and make a better world. The people who called him a power-seeker and a dictator were just the same ones who used to say that Hitler was insane and Nixon was insane and all the world leaders were insane and the arms race was insane and our misuse of natural resources was insane and the whole world civilization was insane and suicidal. They were always saying that. And they said it about Dr. Speakie. But he stopped all that insanity, didn't he? So he was right all along, and he was right to believe in his beliefs.

I came to work for him when he was named the Chief of the Psychometric Bureau. I used to work at the U.N., and when the World Government took over the New York U.N. Building they transferred me up to the thirty-fifth floor to be the head secretary in Dr. Speakie's office. I knew already that it was a position of great responsibility and I was quite excited the whole week before my new job began. I was so curious to meet Dr. Speakie, because of course he was already famous. I was there right at the dot of nine on Monday morning, and when he came in it was so wonderful. He looked so kind. You could tell that the weight of his responsibilities was always on his mind, but he looked so healthy and positive, and there was a bounce in his step—I used to think it was as if he had rubber balls in the toes of his shoes. He smiled and shook my hand and said in such a friendly, confident voice, "And you must be Mrs. Smith! I've heard wonderful things about you. We're going to have a wonderful team here, Mrs. Smith!"

Later on he called me by my first name, of course.

That first year we were mostly busy with information. The World Government Presidium and all the Member States had to be fully informed about the nature and purpose of the SQ Test, before the actual implementation of its application could be eventualized. That was good for me too, because in preparing all that information I learned all about it myself. Often, taking dictation, I learned about it from Dr. Speakie's very lips. By May I was enough of an "expert" that I was able to prepare the Basic SQ Information Pamphlet for publication just from Dr. Speakie's notes. It was such fascinating work. As soon as I began to understand the SQ Test Plan I began to believe in it. That was true of everybody in the office and in the Bureau. Dr. Speakie's sincerity and scientific enthusiasm were infectious. Right from the beginning we had to take the Test every quarter, of course, and some of the secretaries used to be nervous before they took it, but I never was. It was so obvious that the Test was *right*. If you scored under 50 it was nice to know that you were sane, but even if you scored over 50 that was fine too, because then you could be *helped*. And anyway it is always best to know the truth about yourself.

As soon as the Information service was functioning smoothly Dr. Speakie transferred the main thrust of his attention to the implementation of Evaluator training, and planning for the structurization of the Cure Centers, only he changed the name to SQ Achievement Centers. It seemed a very big job even then. We certainly had no idea how big the job would finally turn out to be!

As he said at the beginning, we were a very good team. We all worked hard, but there were always rewards.

I remember one wonderful day. I had accompanied Dr. Speakie to the Meeting of the Board of the Psychometric[1] Bureau. The emissary from

1 **psychometric:** related to the measurement and testing of psychological variables

the State of Brazil announced that his State had adopted the Bureau Recommendations for Universal Testing—we had known that that was going to be announced. But then the delegate from Libya and the delegate from China announced that their States had adopted the test too! Oh, Dr. Speakie's face was just like the sun for a minute, just *shining*. I wish I could remember exactly what he said, especially to the Chinese delegate, because of course China was a very big State and its decision was very influential. Unfortunately I do not have his exact words because I was changing the tape in the recorder. He said something like, "Gentlemen, this is a historic day for humanity." Then he began to talk at once about the effective implementation of the Application Centers, where people would take the Test, and the Achievement Centers, where they would go if they scored over 50, and how to establish the Test Administrations and Evaluations infrastructure[2] on such a large scale, and so on. He was always modest and practical. He would rather talk about doing the job than talk about what an important job it was. He used to say, "Once you know what you're doing, the only thing you need to think about is how to do it." I believe that that is deeply true.

From then on, we could hand over the Information program to a sub-department and concentrate on How to Do It. Those were exciting times! So many States joined the Plan, one after another. When I think of all we had to do I wonder that we didn't all go crazy! Some of the office staff did fail their quarterly Test, in fact. But most of us working in the Executive Office with Dr. Speakie remained quite stable, even when we were on the job all day and half the night. I think his presence was an inspiration. He was always calm and positive, even when we had to arrange things like training 113,000 Chinese Evaluators in three months. "You can always find out 'how' if you just know the 'why'!" he would say. And we always did.

When you think back over it, it really is quite amazing what a big job it was—so much bigger than anybody, even Dr. Speakie, had realized it would be. It just changed everything. You only realize that when you think back to what things used to be like. Can you imag ine when we began planning Universal Testing for the State of China, we only allowed for 1,100 Achievement Centers, with 6,800 Staff?" It really seems like a joke! But it is not. I was going through some of the old files yesterday, making sure everything is in order, and I

2 **infrastructure:** basic equipment, buildings, etc., needed for the functioning of a system

found the first China Implementation Plan, with those figures written down in black and white.

I believe the reason why even Dr. Speakie was slow to realize the magnitude of the operation was that even though he was a great scientist he was also an optimist. He just kept hoping against hope that the average scores would begin to go down, and this prevented him from seeing that universal application of the SQ Test was eventually going to involve everybody either as Inmates or as Staff.

When most of the Russias and all the African States had adopted the Recommendations and were busy implementing them, the debates in the General Assembly of the World Government got very excited. That was the period when so many bad things were said about the Test and about Dr. Speakie. I used to get quite angry, reading the *World Times* reports of debates. When I went as his secretary with Dr. Speakie to General Assembly meetings I had to sit and listen in person to people insulting him personally, casting aspersions on his motives and questioning his scientific integrity and even his sincerity. Many of those people were very disagreeable and obviously unbalanced. But he never lost his temper. He would just stand up and prove to them, again, that the SQ Test did actually literally scientifically show whether the testee was sane or insane, and the results could be proved, and all psychometrists accepted them. So the Test Ban people couldn't do anything but shout about freedom and accuse Dr. Speakie and the Psychometric Bureau of trying to "turn the world into a huge insane asylum." He would always answer quietly and firmly, asking them how they thought a person could be "free" if they lacked mental health. What they called freedom might well be a delusional[3] system with no contact with reality. In order to find out, all they had to do was to become testees. "Mental health *is* freedom," he said. "'Eternal vigilance is the price of liberty,' they say, and now we have an eternally vigilant watchdog: the SQ Test. *Only the testees can be truly free!*"

There really was no answer they could make to that. Sooner or later the delegates even from Member States where the Test Ban movement was strong would volunteer to take the SQ Test to prove that their mental health was adequate to their responsibilities. Then the ones who passed the test and remained in office would begin working for

3 **delusional:** fanciful; mentally unsound

Universal Application in their home State. Riots and demonstrations, and things like the burning of the Houses of Parliament in London in the State of England (where the Nor-Eurp SQ Center was housed) and the Vatican Rebellion, and the Chilean H-bomb, was the work of insane fanatics appealing to the most unstable elements of the populace. Such fanatics, as Dr. Speakie and Dr. Waltraute pointed out in their Memorandum to the Presidium, deliberately aroused and used the proven instability of the crowd, "mob psychosis." The only response to mass delusion of that kind was immediate implementation of the Testing Program in the disturbed States, and immediate amplification of the Asylum Program.

That was Dr. Speakie's own decision, by the way, to rename the SQ Achievement Centers "Asylums." He took the word right out of his enemies' mouths. He said: "An asylum means a place of *shelter*; a place of *cure*. Let there be no stigma attached to the word 'insane,' to the word 'asylum,' to the words 'insane asylum'! No! For the asylum is the haven of mental health—the place of cure, where the anxious gain peace, where the weak gain strength, where the prisoners of inadequate reality assessment win their way to freedom! Proudly let us use the word 'asylum.' Proudly let us go to the asylum, to work to regain our own God-given mental health, or to work with others less fortunate to help them win back their own inalienable[4] right to mental health. And let one word be written large over the door of every asylum in the world—'WELCOME!' "

Those words are from his great speech at the General Assembly on the day World Universal Application was decreed by the Presidium. Once or twice a year I listen to my tape of that speech. Although I am too busy ever to get really depressed, now and then I feel the need of a tiny "pick-me-up," and so I play that tape. It never fails to send me back to my duties inspired and refreshed.

Considering all the work there was to do, as the Test scores continued to come in always a little higher than the Psychometric Bureau analysts estimated, the World Government Presidium did a wonderful job for the two years that it administered Universal Testing. There was a long period, six months, when the scores seemed to have stabilized, with just about half of the testees scoring over 50 and half under 50. At that time it was thought that if forty percent of the mentally healthy were assigned

4 **inalienable:** not transferable to another

to Asylum Staff work, the other sixty percent could keep up routine basic world functions such as farming, power supply, transportation, etc. This proportion had to be reversed when they found that over sixty percent of the mentally healthy were volunteering for Staff work, in order to be with their loved ones in the Asylums. There was some trouble then with the routine basic world functions functioning. However, even then contingency plans were being made for the inclusion of farmlands, factories, power plants, etc., in the Asylum Territories, and the assignment of routine basic world functions work as Rehabilitation Therapy, so that the Asylums could become totally self-supporting if it became advisable. This was President Kim's special care, and he worked for it all through his term of office. Events proved the wisdom of his planning. He seemed such a nice wise little man. I still remember the day when Dr. Speakie came into the office and I knew at once that something was wrong. Not that he ever got really depressed or reacted with inopportune[5] emotion, but it was as if the rubber balls in his shoes had gone just a little bit flat. There was the slightest tremor of true sorrow in his voice when he said, "Mary Ann, we've had a bit of bad news, I'm afraid." Then he smiled to reassure me, because he knew what a strain we were all working under, and certainly didn't want to give anybody a shock that might push their score up higher on the next quarterly Tests. "It's President Kim," he said, and I knew at once—I knew he didn't mean the President was ill or dead.

"Over fifty?" I asked, and he just said quietly, sadly, "Fifty-five."

Poor little President Kim, working so efficiently that three months while mental ill health was growing in him! It was very sad and also a useful warning. High-level consultations were begun at once, as soon as President Kim was committed; and the decision was made to administer the Test monthly, instead of quarterly, to anyone in an executive position.

Even before this decision, the Universal scores had begun rising again. Dr. Speakie was not distressed. He had already predicted that this rise was highly probable during the transition period to World Sanity. As the number of the mentally healthy living outside the Asylums grew fewer, the strain on them kept growing greater, and they became more liable to break down under it—just as poor President Kim had done. Later, he predicted, when the Rehabs began coming out of the Asylums in ever increasing numbers, this stress would decrease. Also the crowding in the Asylums would decrease, so that the Staff would have more time to work

5 **inopportune:** inconvenient

on individually orientated therapy, and this would lead to a still more dramatic increase in the number of Rehabs released. Finally, when the therapy process was completely perfected, there would be no Asylums left in the world at all. Everybody would be either mentally healthy or a Rehab, or "neonormal,"[6] as Dr Speakie liked to call it.

It was the trouble in the State of Australia that precipitated the Government crisis. Some Psychometric Bureau officials accused the Australian Evaluators of actually falsifying Test returns, but that is impossible since all the computers are linked to the World Government Central Computer Bank in Keokuk. Dr. Speakie suspected that the Australian Evaluators had been falsifying *the Test itself*, and insisted that they themselves all be tested immediately. Of course he was right. It had been a conspiracy, and the suspiciously low Australian Test scores had resulted from the use of a false Test. Many of the conspirators tested higher than 80 when forced to take the genuine Test! The State Government in Canberra had been unforgivably lax. If they had just admitted it everything would have been all right. But they got hysterical, and moved the State Government to a sheep station in Queensland, and tried to withdraw from the World Government. (Dr. Speakie said this was a typical mass psychosis: reality evasion, followed by fugue[7] and autistic withdrawal.) Unfortunately the Presidium seemed to be paralyzed. Australia seceded on the day before the President and Presidium were due to take their monthly Test, and probably they were afraid of overstraining their SQ with agonizing decisions. So the Psychometric Bureau volunteered to handle the episode. Dr. Speakie himself flew on the plane with the H-bombs, and helped to drop the information leaflets. He never lacked personal courage.

When the Australian incident was over, it turned out that most of the Presidium, including President Singh, had scored over 50. So the Psychometric Bureau took over their functions temporarily. Even on a long-term basis this made good sense, since all the problems now facing the World Government had to do with administering and evaluating the Test, training the Staff, and providing full self-sufficiency structuration to all Asylums.

What this meant in personal terms was that Dr. Speakie, as Chief of

6 **neonormal:** a coined word combining the prefix *neo*, which means new, with the word *normal*—newly normal

7 **fugue:** a condition during which an individual is apparently aware of his actions but has no recollection of them later

the Psychometric Bureau, was now Interim President of the United States of the World. As his personal secretary I was, I will admit it, just terribly proud of him. But he never let it go to his head.

He was so modest. Sometimes he used to say to people, when he introduced me, "This is Mary Ann, my secretary," he'd say with a little twinkle, "and if it wasn't for her I'd have been scoring over fifty long ago!"

There were times, as the World SQ scores rose and rose, that I would become a little discouraged. Once the week's Test figures came in on the readout, and the *average* score was 71. I said, "Doctor, there are moments I believe the whole world is going insane!"

But he said, "Look at it this way, Mary Ann. Look at those people in the Asylums—3.1 billion inmates now, and 1.8 billion staff—but look at them. What are they doing? They're pursuing their therapy, doing rehabilitation work on the farms and in the factories, and striving all the time, too, to *help* each other towards mental health. The preponderant inverse sanity quotient is certainly very high at the moment; they're mostly insane, yes. But you have to admire them. They are fighting for mental health. They will—they *will* win through!" And then he dropped his voice and said as if to himself, gazing out the window and bouncing just a little on the balls of his feet, "If I didn't believe that, I couldn't go on."

And I knew he was thinking of his wife.

Mrs. Speakie had scored 88 on the very first American Universal Test. She had been in the Greater Los Angeles Territory Asylum for years now.

Anybody who still thinks Dr. Speakie wasn't sincere should think about that for a minute! He gave up everything for his belief.

And even when the Asylums were all running quite well, and the epidemics in South Africa and the famines in Texas and the Ukraine were under control, still the workload on Dr. Speakie never got any lighter, because every month the personnel of the Psychometric Bureau got smaller, since some of them always flunked their monthly Test and were committed to Bethesda. I never could keep any of my secretarial staff any more for longer than a month or two. It was harder and harder to find replacements, too, because most sane young people volunteered for Staff work in the Asylums, since life was much easier and more sociable inside the Asylums than outside. Everything so convenient, and lots of friends and acquaintances! I used to positively envy those girls! But I knew where my job was.

At least it was much less hectic here in the U.N. Building, or the Psychometry Tower as it had been renamed long ago. Often there wouldn't be anybody around the whole building all day long but Dr. Speakie and myself, and maybe Bill the janitor (Bill scored 32 regular as clockwork every quarter). All the restaurants were closed, in fact most of Manhattan was closed, but we had fun picnicking in the old General Assembly Hall. And there was always the odd call from Buenos Aires or Reykjavik, asking Dr. Speakie's advice as Interim President about some problem, to break the silence.

But last November 8, I will never forget the date, when Dr. Speakie was dictating the Referendum for World Economic Growth for the next five-year period, he suddenly interrupted himself. "By the way, Mary Ann," he said, "how was your last score?"

We had taken the Test two days before, on the sixth. We always took the Test every first Monday. Dr. Speakie never would have dreamed of excepting himself from Universal Testing regulations.

"I scored twelve," I said, before I thought how strange it was of him to ask. Or, not just to ask, because we often mentioned our scores to each other, but to ask *then*, in the middle of executing important World Government business.

"Wonderful," he said, shaking his head. "You're wonderful, Mary Ann! Down two from last month's Test, aren't you?"

"I'm always between ten and fourteen," I said. "Nothing new about that, Doctor."

"Some day," he said, and his face took on the expression it had when he gave his great speech about the Asylums, "some day, this world of ours will be governed by men fit to govern it. Men whose SQ score is zero. Zero, Mary Ann!"

"Well, my goodness, Doctor," I said jokingly—his intensity almost alarmed me a little—"even *you* never scored lower than three, and you haven't done that for a year or more now!"

He stared at me almost as if he didn't see me. It was quite uncanny. "Some day," he said in just the same way, "nobody in the world will have a Quotient higher than fifty. Some day, nobody in the world will have a Quotient higher than thirty! Higher than ten! The Therapy will be perfected. I was only the diagnostician. But the Therapy will be perfected!

The cure will be found! Some day!" And he went on staring at me, and then he said, "Do you know what my score was on Monday?"

"Seven," I guessed promptly. The last time he had told me his score it had been seven.

"Ninety-two," he said.

I laughed, because he seemed to be laughing. He had always had a puckish sense of humor. But I thought we really should get back to the World Economic Growth Plan, so I said laughingly, "That really is a very bad joke, Doctor!"

"Ninety-two," he said, "and you don't believe me, Mary Ann, but that's because of the cantaloupe."

I said, "What cantaloupe, Doctor?" and that was when he jumped across his desk and began to try to bite through my jugular vein.

I used a judo hold and shouted to Bill the janitor, and when he came I called a robo-ambulance to take Dr. Speakie to Bethesda Asylum.

That was six months ago. I visit Dr. Speakie every Saturday. It is very sad. He is in the McLean Area, which is the Violent Ward, and every time he sees me he screams and foams. But I do not take it personally. One should never take mental ill health personally. When the Therapy is perfected he will be completely rehabilitated. Meanwhile, I just hold on here. Bill keeps the floors clean, and I run the World Government. It really isn't as difficult as you might think.

All Watched Over by Machines of Loving Grace

Richard Brautigan

I like to think (and
the sooner the better!)
of a cybernetic[1] meadow
where mammals and computers
live together in mutually
programming harmony
like pure water
touching clear sky.

I like to think
(right now, please!)
of a cybernetic forest
filled with pines and electronics
where deer stroll peacefully
past computers
as if they were flowers
with spinning blossoms.

I like to think
(it has to be!)
of a cybernetic ecology
where we are free of our labors
and joined back to nature,
returned to our mammal
brothers and sisters,
and all watched over
by machines of loving grace.

1 **cybernetic:** related to the analysis of the flow of information in electronic, mechanical, or biological systems

Minister Without Portfolio

MILDRED CLINGERMAN

Mrs. Chriswell's little roadster came to a shuddering halt. Here was the perfect spot. Only one sagging wire fence to step over and not a cow in sight. Mrs. Chriswell was terrified of cows, and if the truth were told, only a little less afraid of her daughter-in-law, Clara. It was all Clara's idea that her mother-in-law should now be lurking in meadows peering at birds. Clara had been delighted with the birdwatching idea, but frankly, Mrs. Chriswell was bored with birds. They *flew* so much. And as for their colours, it was useless for her to speculate. Mrs. Chriswell was one of those rare women who are quite, quite colour-blind.

"But, Clara," Mrs. Chriswell had pleaded, "what's the point if I can't tell what colour they are?"

"Well, but, darling," Clara had said crisply, "how much cleverer if you get to know them just from the distinctive markings!"

Mrs. Chriswell, sighing a little as she recalled the firm look of Clara's chin, manoeuvred herself and her burdens over the sagging wire fence. She successfully juggled the binoculars, the heavy bird book, and her purse, and thought how ghastly it was at sixty to be considered so useless that she must be provided with harmless occupations to keep her out of the way.

Since Mr. Chriswell's death she had moved in with her son and his wife to face a life of enforced idleness. The servants resented her presence in the kitchen, so cooking was out. Clara and the snooty nursemaid would brook no interference with the nursery routine, so

Mrs. Chriswell had virtually nothing to do. Even her crocheted doilies disappeared magically soon after their presentation to Clara and the modern furniture.

Mrs. Chriswell shifted the heavy bird book and considered rebelling. The sun was hot and her load was heavy. As she toiled on across the field she thought she saw the glint of sun on water. She would sit and crochet in the shade nearby and remove the big straw cartwheel hat Clara termed "just the thing."

Arrived at the trees, Mrs. Chriswell dropped her burdens and flung the hat willy-nilly. Ugly, ridiculous thing. She glanced around for the water she thought she'd seen, but there was no sign of it. She leaned back against a tree trunk and sighed blissfully. A little breeze had sprung up and was cooling the damp tendrils on her forehead. She opened her big purse and scrambled through the muddle of contents for her crochet hook and the ball of thread attached to a half-finished doily. In her search she came across the snapshots of her granddaughters—in colour, they were, but unfortunately Mrs. Chriswell saw them only in various shades of grey. The breeze was getting stronger now, very pleasant, but the dratted old cartwheel monstrosity was rolling merrily down the slight grade to the tangle of berry bushes a few yards away. Well, it would catch on the brambles. But it didn't. The wind flirted it right around the bushes, and the hat disappeared.

"Fiddle!" Mrs. Chriswell dared not face Clara without the hat. Still hanging on to the bulky purse, she got up to give chase. Rounding the tangle of bushes, she ran smack into a tall young man in uniform.

"Oh!" Mrs. Chriswell said. "Have you seen my hat?"

The young man smiled and pointed on down the hill. Mrs. Chriswell was surprised to see her hat being passed from hand to hand among three other tall young men in uniform. They were laughing at it, and she didn't much blame them. They were standing beside a low, silvery aircraft of some unusual design. Mrs. Chriswell studied it a moment, but, really, she knew nothing about such things. . . . The sun glinted off it, and she realized this was what she had thought was water. The young man beside her touched her arm. She turned towards him and saw that he had put a rather lovely little metal hat on his head. He offered her one with grave courtesy. Mrs. Chriswell smiled up at him and nodded. The young man fitted the hat carefully, adjusting various little ornamental knobs on the top of it.

"Now we can talk," he said. "Do you hear well?"

"My dear boy," Mrs. Chriswell said, "of course I do. I'm not so old as all that." She found a smooth stone and sat down to chat. This was much nicer than birdwatching, or even crochet.

The tall young man grinned and signalled excitedly to his companions. They too put on little metal hats and came bounding up the hill. Still laughing, they deposited the cartwheel in Mrs. Chriswell's lap. She patted the stone by way of invitation, and the youngest looking one of the four dropped down beside her.

"What is your name, Mother?" he asked.

"Ida Chriswell," she said. "What's yours?"

"My name is Jord," the boy said.

Mrs. Chriswell patted his hand. "That's a nice, unusual name." The boy grabbed Mrs. Chriswell's hand and rubbed it against the smoothness of his cheek.

"You are like my Mother's Mother," the boy explained, "whom I have not seen in too long." The other young men laughed, and the boy looked abashed and stealthily wiped with his hands at a tear that slid down his nose.

Mrs. Chriswell frowned warningly at the laughter and handed him her clean pocket handkerchief, scented with lavender. Jord turned it over and over in his hands, and then tentatively sniffed at it.

"It's all right," Mrs. Chriswell said. "Use it. I have another." But Jord only breathed more deeply of the faint perfume in its fold.

"This is only the thinnest thread of melody," he said, "but, Mother Ida, it is very like one note from the Harmony Hills of home!" He passed the handkerchief all around the circle, and the young men sniffed at it and smiled.

Mrs. Chriswell tried to remember if she had ever read of the Harmony Hills, but Mr. Chriswell had always told her she was lamentably weak in geography, and she supposed that this was one of her blank spots, like where on earth was Timbuktu? Or the Hellandgone people were always talking about? But it was rude not to make some comment. Wars shifted people about such a lot, and these boys must be homesick and weary of being strangers, longing to talk of home. She was proud of herself for realizing that they were strangers. But there was something. . . . Hard to say, really. The way they had bounded up the hill? Mountain people, perhaps, to whom hills were mere springboards to heights beyond.

"Tell me about your hills," she said.

"Wait," Jord said. "I will show you." He glanced at his leader as if for approval. The young man who had fitted her hat nodded. Jord drew a fingernail across the breast of his uniform. Mrs. Chriswell was surprised to see a pocket opening where no pocket had been before. Really, the Air Force did amazing things with its uniforms, though, frankly, Mrs. Chriswell thought the cut of these a bit extreme.

Carefully, Jord was lifting out a packet of gossamer material. He gently pressed the centre of the packet and it blossomed out into voluminous clouds of featherweight threads, held loosely together in a wave like a giant spider web. To Mrs. Chriswell's eyes the mesh of threads was the colour of fog, and almost as insubstantial.

"Do not be afraid," Jord said softly, stepping closer to her. "Bend your head, close your eyes, and you shall hear the lovely Harmony Hills of home."

There was one quick-drawn breath of almost-fear, but before she shut her eyes Mrs. Chriswell saw the love in Jord's, and in that moment she knew how rarely she had seen this look, anywhere . . . anytime. If Jord had asked it of her, it was all right. She closed her eyes and bowed her head, and in that attitude of prayer she felt a soft weightlessness descend upon her. It was as if twilight had come down to drape itself on her shoulders. And then the music began. Behind the darkness of her eyes it rose in majesty and power, in colours she had never seen, never guessed. It blossomed like flowers—giant forests of them. Their scents were intoxicating and filled her with joy. She could not tell if the blending perfumes made the music, or if the music itself created the flowers and the perfumes that poured forth from them. She did not care. She wanted only to go on forever listening to all this colour. It seemed odd to be listening to colour, perhaps, but after all, she told herself, it would seem just as odd to me to *see* it.

She sat blinking at the circle of young men. The music was finished. Jord was putting away the gossamer threads in the secret pocket, and laughing aloud at her astonishment.

"Did you like it, Mother Ida?" he dropped down beside her again and patted her wrinkled face, still pink with excitement.

"Oh, Jord," she said, "how lovely . . . Tell me . . ."

But the leader was calling them all to order. "I'm sorry, Mother Ida, we must hurry about our business. Will you answer some questions? It is very important."

"Of course," Mrs. Chriswell said. She was still feeling a bit dazed.

"If I can . . . If it's like the quizzes on the TV, though, I'm not very good at it."

The young man shook his head. "We," he said, "have been instructed to investigate and report on the true conditions of this . . . of the world." He pointed at the aircraft glittering in the sunlight. "We have travelled all around in that slow machine, and our observations have been accurate. . . ." He hesitated, drew a deep breath and continued. ". . . and perhaps we shall be forced to give an unfavourable report, but this depends a great deal on the outcome of our talk with you. We are glad you stumbled upon us. We were about to set out on a foray[1] to secure some individual for questioning. It is our last task." He smiled. "And Jord, here, will not be sorry. He is sick for home and loved ones." He sighed, and all the other young men echoed the sigh.

"Every night," Mrs. Chriswell said, "I pray for peace on earth. I cannot bear to think of boys like you fighting and dying, and the folks at home waiting and waiting . . ." She glanced all around at their listening faces. "And I'll tell you something else," she said, "I find I can't really hate anybody, even the enemy." Around the circle the young men nodded at each other. "Now ask me your questions." She fumbled in her purse for her crochet work and found it.

Beside her Jord exclaimed with pleasure at the sight of the half-finished doily. Mrs. Chriswell warmed to him even more.

The tall young man began his grave questioning. They were very simple questions, and Mrs. Chriswell answered them without hesitation. Did she believe in God? Did she believe in the dignity of man? Did she truly abhor war? Did she believe that man was capable of love for his neighbour? The questions went on and on, and Mrs. Chriswell crocheted while she gave her answers.

At last, when the young man had quite run out of questions, and Mrs. Chriswell had finished the doily, Jord broke the sun-lazy silence that had fallen upon them.

"May I have it, Mother?" He pointed to the doily. Mrs. Chriswell bestowed it upon him with great pleasure, and Jord, like a very small boy, stuffed it greedily into another secret pocket. He pointed at her stuffed purse.

"May I look, Mother?"

Mrs. Chriswell indulgently passed him her purse. He opened it and poured the litter of contents on the ground between them. The snapshots of Mrs. Chriswell's grandchildren stared up at him. Jord smiled at the

1 **foray:** raid; military action

pretty little-girl faces. He groped in the chest pocket and drew out snapshots of his own. "These," he told Mrs. Chriswell proudly, "are my little sisters. Are they not like these little girls of yours? Let us exchange, because soon I will be at home with them, and there will be no need for pictures. I would like to have yours."

Mrs. Chriswell would have given Jord the entire contents of the purse if he had asked for them. She took the snapshots he offered and looked with pleasure at the sweet-faced children. Jord still stirred at the pile of possessions from Mrs. Chriswell's purse. By the time she was ready to leave he had talked her out of three illustrated recipes torn from magazines, some swatches of material, and two pieces of peppermint candy.

The young man who was the leader helped her to remove the pretty little hat when Mrs. Chriswell indicated he should. She would have liked to keep it, but she didn't believe Clara would approve. She clapped the straw monstrosity on her head, kissed Jord's cheek, waved goodbye to the rest, and groped her way around the berry bushes. She had to grope because her eyes were tear-filled. They had saluted her so grandly as she left.

Clara's usually sedate household was in an uproar when Mrs. Chriswell returned. All the radios in the house were blaring. Even Clara sat huddled over the one in the library. Mrs. Chriswell heard a boy in the street crying "EXTRA! EXTRA!" and the upstairs maid almost knocked her down getting out the front door to buy one. Mrs. Chriswell, sleepy and somewhat sunburned, supposed it was something about the awful war.

She was just turning up the stairs to her room when the snooty nursemaid came rushing down to disappear kitchenwards with another newspaper in her hand. Good, the children were alone. She'd stop in to see them. Suddenly she heard the raised voices from the back of the house. The cook was yelling at somebody. "I tell you, I saw it! I took out some garbage and there it was, right over me!" Mrs. Chriswell lingered at the foot of the stairway puzzled by all the confusion. The housemaid came rushing in with the extra edition. Mrs. Chriswell quietly reached out and took it. "Thank you, Nadine," she said. The nursemaid was still staring at her as she climbed the stairs.

Edna and Evelyn were sitting on the nursery floor, a candy box between them, and shrieking at each other when their grandmother opened the door. They were cramming chocolates into their mouths between shrieks. Their faces and pinafores[2] were smeared with the candy. Edna suddenly yanked Evelyn's hair, hard. "Pig!" she shouted. "You got three more than I did!"

"Children! Children! Not fighting?" Mrs. Chriswell was delighted. Here was something she could cope with. She led them firmly to the bathroom and washed their faces. "Change your frocks," she said, "and I'll tell you my adventure."

There were only hissing accusals and whispered countercharges behind her as she turned her back on the children to scan the newspaper. The headlines leapt up at her.

Mysterious broadcast interrupts programmes on all wave lengths

Unknown woman saves world, say men from space

One sane human found on earth

Cooking, needlework, home, religious interests sway space judges

Every column of the paper was crowded with the same unintelligible nonsense. Mrs. Chriswell folded it neatly, deposited it on the table, and turned to tie her granddaughters' sashes and tell her adventure.

". . . And then he gave me some lovely photographs. In colour, he said . . . Good little girls, just like Edna and Evelyn. Would you like to see them?"

Edna made a rude noise with her mouth pursed. Evelyn's face grew saintlike in retaliation. "Yes, show us," she said.

Mrs. Chriswell passed them the snapshots, and the children drew close together for the moment before Evelyn dropped the pictures as if they were blazing. She stared hard at her grandmother while Edna made a gagging nose.

"Green!" Edna gurgled. "Gaaa . . . green skins!"

"Grandmother!" Evelyn was tearful. "Those children are frog-coloured!"

Mrs. Chriswell bent over to pick up the pictures. "Now, now, children," she murmured absently. "We don't worry about the colour of people's skins. Red . . . yellow . . . black . . . we're all God's children. Asia or Africa, makes no difference . . ." But before she could finish her thought, the nursemaid loomed disapprovingly in the doorway. Mrs. Chriswell hurried out to her own room, while some tiny worry nagged at her mind. "Red, yellow, black, white," she murmured over and over, "and brown . . . but green . . . ?" Geography had always been her weak point. Green . . . Now where on earth . . . ?

2 **pinafores:** sleeveless garments worn by young girls as overdresses

The Choice

W. HILTON-YOUNG

Before Williams went into the future he bought a camera and a tape recording machine and learned shorthand. That night, when all was ready, we made coffee and put out brandy and glasses against his return.

"Good-bye," I said. "Don't stay too long."

"I won't," he answered.

I watched him carefully, and he hardly flickered. He must have made a perfect landing on the very second he had taken off from. He seemed not a day older; we had expected he might spend several years away.

"Well?"

"Well," said he, "let's have some coffee."

I poured it out, hardly able to contain my impatience. As I gave it to him I said again, "Well?"

"Well, the thing is, I can't remember."

"Can't remember? Not a thing?"

He thought for a moment and answered sadly, "Not a thing."

"But your notes? The camera? The recording machine?"

The notebook was empty, the indicator of the camera rested at "1" where we had set it, the tape was not even loaded into the recording machine.

"But good heavens," I protested, "why? How did it happen? Can you remember nothing at all?"

"I can remember only one thing."

"What was that?"

"I was shown everything, and I was given the choice whether I should remember it or not after I got back."

"And you chose not to? But what an extraordinary thing to—"

"Isn't it?" he said. "One can't help wondering why."

Responding to Cluster Four

Thinking Skill SYNTHESIS

1. Each of the other clusters in this book is introduced by a question that is meant to help readers focus their thinking about the selections. What do you think the question for cluster four should be?

2. How do you think the selections in this cluster should be taught? Demonstrate your ideas by joining with your classmates to:

   a) create discussion questions

   b) lead discussions about the selections

   c) develop vocabulary quizzes

   d) prepare a cluster test

Reflecting on the Sci-Fi Factor

Essential Question WHAT'S THE FASCINATION WITH SCIENCE FICTION?

Reflecting on this book as a whole provides an opportunity for independent learning and the application of the critical thinking skill called *synthesis*. Synthesizing means examining all the things you have learned from this book and combining them to form a greater understanding of the science fiction genre and its appeal for millions of readers.

There are many ways to demonstrate what you know about science fiction. Here are some possibilities. Your teacher may provide others.

1. After reading this book you should have a better idea of the broad range of literature that can be included in the science fiction category. You should also have some well-formed positions on your reading preferences regarding this genre. As you read, your position may have changed from positive to negative or vice versa or you may have decided that you liked certain sci-fi authors but not others. Write an essay that states your opinion about reading science fiction. Start with an opinion statement such as "Reading science fiction is __________. (silly, fun, a waste of time, a great escape, fascinating, boring, etc.) Back up your opinion with reasons that explain why you feel as you do and with plenty of examples from the selections.

2. Individually or in small groups, develop an independent project that demonstrates your knowledge of and ideas about science fiction. Options might include research, music, dance, drama, original art, creating a sci-fi art gallery, building a mini-library of sci-fi favorites, planning a sci-fi film festival, or writing and reading aloud your own sci-fi story or poem.

CLOSE READING

Re-reading, we find a new book. —Mason Cooley

Close reading is the careful interpretation of a text. Re-reading is the key strategy for close reading. The "new book" readers often encounter on re-reading is layered with meaning.

There is no single right way to do a close reading of a text. The following general process, however, presents three broad stages or levels in re-reading that build on one another to help produce a deep understanding of a text.

1. First Readings: Build Understanding

On a first reading, focus on grasping the literal or explicit meaning of a text. Answer the questions as you read, paraphrase key ideas, and jot down any questions you have.

Informational Text	
Questions to Ask	**Where to Look for Answers**
What is the main idea?	Title, introduction, or first few paragraphs
What information backs up the main idea?	Body paragraphs, especially their topic sentences
How are the ideas in the text related to one another?	Transitions between sections/ideas
What conclusion does the writer draw, and how does it relate to the main idea and supporting ideas?	Concluding paragraphs

Argumentative Text	
Questions to Ask	**Where to Look for Answers**
What is the main claim, or point the writer is trying to prove?	Title, introduction, or first few paragraphs
What evidence does the writer provide to back up that claim?	Body paragraphs, especially their topic sentences
What counterclaims, if any, does the writer address?	Body paragraphs, often marked with such words and phrases as "in contrast," "despite," "while it is true that"
How are the ideas in the text related to one another?	Transitions between sections/ideas
What conclusion does the writer draw, and how does it relate to the main claim and supporting ideas?	Concluding paragraphs

Narrative Text	
Questions to Ask	**Where to Look for Answers**
What event starts the narrative in motion?	Introduction or first few paragraphs
What is the setting of the narrative?	Introduction and throughout
Who are the people or characters in the narrative?	Introduction and throughout
What problem do the people or characters face?	Introduction and throughout
What happens to the people or characters as the narrative unfolds?	Body paragraphs
What is the outcome or resolution of the narrative?	Concluding paragraphs

Poetry	
Questions to Ask	**Where to Look for Answers**
If the poem tells a story, what is the basic outline of that story?	Throughout
What is the tone of the poem?	Throughout
What images, words, or ideas stand out as striking?	Throughout
What images, words, or ideas are repeated, if any?	Throughout
What message do you see in the poem?	Title, throughout

2. Focused Re-readings: Analyze the Text and Gather Evidence

Re-reading after you have grasped a basic understanding of a text is the stage at which you are most likely to encounter that "new book" referred to in the beginning quote, because at this level you analyze the text carefully and focus on details that may bring new meaning to what you have read. The chart below shows some of the points you can focus on in a re-reading of almost any kind of text. It also shows what questions you can ask and where and how you can discover the answers to those questions.

Focused Re-reading		
Focus and Thinking Skills	**Questions to Ask**	**Finding Textual Evidence**
Author's purpose, such as to inform, put forward an argument, entertain, satirize, tell a story *Thinking skills: Recognize explicit statements; draw inferences about implied purpose(s)*	Why did the writer write this? Is the purpose stated explicitly or is it only implied?	Look in the title and beginning paragraphs for quotes that show the answers to your questions.

continued

Focused Re-reading *(cont.)*		
Focus and Thinking Skills	**Questions to Ask**	**Finding Textual Evidence**
Word choice and style, including length of sentences, variety of sentence beginnings, and variety of sentence types *Thinking skills: Analyze; break passages down by word choice and sentence style and look for patterns*	What words and phrases caught your attention for their strength and clarity? Does the author tend to use long sentences, short sentences, or a variety of sentence lengths? Do the sentences begin in a variety of ways (for example, subject first, prepositional phrase first, etc.)?	Look throughout for examples that demonstrate the results of your analysis (for example, three vivid word choices, three varied sentence patterns, etc.). In a long text, examine a section from the beginning, two or three sections from the middle, and a section from the end.
Figurative language, such as similes, metaphors, hyperbole, alliteration *Thinking skills: Analyze to identify figures of speech; classify the type of figurative language; compare figurative language to a possible replacement in literal language*	What figures of speech does the writer use? What do they accomplish that literal language would not?	Look throughout, but especially in descriptive passages, for various examples of figurative language and compare them to literal language.
Structure, including main sections and such organizational patterns as chronological order and order of importance *Thinking skills: Analyze to identify the sections of a text; classify to determine the organizational pattern*	What are the main sections of the text? What is the organizational pattern of the text?	Look throughout the text for transitional words and phrases that show both where sections break and how they are connected. Identify the main ideas from each section.
Point of view in fiction, including choice of narrator *Thinking skills: Analyze narrative to identify point of view; compare points of view by imagining a passage told from a different point of view and evaluating the effect.*	Is the story told from the first- or third-person point of view? If it is not in first-person, how much does the narrator know about the characters? What effect does the choice of narrative point of view have on the text? Why might the author have chosen that point of view?	Look for pronouns. If the narrator refers to himself or herself as "I," the story is in first-person. Look at key passages in which important information is revealed for examples that show the effect of point of view on the narrative.

continued

Focused Re-reading *(cont.)*		
Focus and Thinking Skills	**Questions to Ask**	**Finding Textual Evidence**
Point of view in nonfiction, including frame of reference, such as scientist, parent, teenager *Thinking skills: Recognize explicit statements; draw inferences about the writer from telling details*	What is the writer's frame of reference?	Look in the introduction and body paragraphs for details that give insight into the writer's experience, worldview, and possible bias.
Implied meanings *Thinking skills: Analyze details; draw inferences and conclusions*	What is left unsaid? What inference can you draw from a collection of details when you "read between the lines"?	Look throughout for details that "show" not "tell." In fiction these would include the actions of the characters and details of the setting. In nonfiction, these might appear in descriptive passages where the reader is left to draw his or her own conclusions. Find examples that support your interpretation of the implied meaning.

Different kinds of texts suggest additional points to focus on during re-reading.

Focused Re-Reading of Informational and Argumentative Text		
Focus and Thinking Skills	**Questions to Ask**	**Finding Textual Evidence**
Clarification and verification of information *Thinking skills: Define key terms; analyze complicated sentences and paragraphs; compare to other sources to verify information*	What parts confused you? What did you not understand well on first reading? What seemed to contradict information you thought you knew?	Look in passages that raised questions in your mind in first reading; refer to outside sources if necessary for confirming or contradicting information.
Assumptions *Thinking skills: Logical thinking to evaluate the assumption underlying the claim*	Does every claim depend on a valid assumption?	Look for passages that put forward claims in an argument; look for examples, if any, of hidden assumptions.

continued

Focused Re-Reading of Informational and Argumentative Text *(cont.)*		
Focus and Thinking Skills	**Questions to Ask**	**Finding Textual Evidence**
Development of an argument and key supporting ideas *Thinking skills: Evaluate the relevance, sufficiency, and importance of the supporting details; distinguish fact from opinion*	By what method does the writer attempt to prove his or her point? Are the supporting ideas relevant and sufficient to prove the point?	Look throughout for all the facts, reasons, and examples offered in support of each claim and/or counterclaim.
Style and tone *Thinking skills: Analyze language choices; evaluate appropriateness*	Is the style formal and respectful, or informal and full of "loaded" language (words that carry strong, usually negative connotations)?	Look throughout, but especially at the beginning and ending where the author wants to make his or her point most strongly, for examples that show formal, respectful language or disrespectful loaded language.

Focused Re-reading of Fiction and Drama		
Focus and Thinking Skills	**Questions to Ask**	**Finding Textual Evidence**
Plot *Thinking skills: Sequence; draw inferences; examine cause-effect relationships*	What is the impact of each main development of the plot on the characters?	Look for examples of characters' words or actions before a turning point in the story and after a turning point.
Setting *Thinking skills: Draw inferences*	How does the setting contribute to the mood of the story? How do the details of the setting help define characters?	Look for descriptive details throughout the story about the time and physical characteristics of the place of the events and their impact on mood and characters.
Characters *Thinking skills: Analyze details of characterization; generalize from details; draw inferences from details*	How does each character contribute to the development of the plot? How do the details of characterization and the dialogue reveal the characters' personalities and motivations? Why do characters act as they do?	Look throughout for character 1) descriptions, 2) thoughts, 3) words, 4) actions, 5) changes, 6) motivations.
Theme *Thinking skills: Draw inferences; generalize from details; synthesize various elements*	How does the author communicate the theme through the development of setting, characters, and plot? What passages and details in the story best express the main theme?	Look for passages and details from each main part of the story or drama that express theme.

Focused Re-reading of Poetry		
Focus and Thinking Skills	**Questions to Ask**	**Finding Textual Evidence**
Persona (the poet's "voice") *Thinking skills: Analyze; draw inferences*	How does the persona relate to the subject, mood, and theme of the poem?	Look for specific examples that show the persona's involvement and reveal attitudes.
Meter and rhyme *Thinking skills: Analyze meter and rhyme; synthesize to assess their effect*	How do the meter and rhyme affect the rhythm and mood of the poem?	Look for metrical patterns and rhyme schemes from several places in the poem.
Sound devices, such as alliteration, assonance, onomatopoeia *Thinking skills: Analyze language; classify types of sound devices; draw inferences about their meaning and effect*	What sound devices are in the poem? What effect do they have?	Look throughout the poem for examples of sound devices in relation to other elements of the poem.
Theme *Thinking skills: Draw inferences; generalize from details; synthesize various elements*	How does the poet communicate the theme through the details of the poem?	Look for passages and details from throughout the poem that express theme.

3. Synthesis: Evaluate the Text

By now you may have encountered the "new book" that close reading often reveals, a text with layers of meaning. On later re-readings, you can stand back from the text and begin to see it from a critic's point of view. Following are some of the criteria by which any great work of literature, or classic, is usually judged. When you evaluate a literary work, nonfiction or fiction, consider the following characteristics.

Some Characteristics of Great Literature
• Explores great themes in human nature and the human experience that many people can identify with—such as growing up, family life, personal struggles, or war • Expresses universal values—such as truth or hope—to which people from many different backgrounds and cultures can relate • Conveys a timeless message that remains true for many generations of readers • Presents vivid impressions of characters, settings, and situations that many generations of readers can treasure • Demonstrates outstanding and inventive understanding of important aspects of humanity and society

The chart below shows some questions you can ask—and answer with evidence from the text—when you are evaluating a text.

Questions for Evaluating a Text	
Informational Text	How effectively has the writer • presented a clear explanation on a topic of value • used examples and other supporting details • accurately conveyed information • structured the explanation • used language and style to add clarity and life • presented an unbiased view • engaged the reader
Argumentative Writing	How effectively has the writer • presented a clear position or claim on a subject of importance • used examples and other details to support claims • accurately conveyed information • addressed counterclaims • used logic • covered the topic in sufficient depth and breadth • been fair-minded • structured the argument • used language and style to add clarity and life • convinced you
Fiction and Drama	How effectively has the writer • drawn well-rounded characters worth getting to know • developed and paced a plot • set mood and tone • used language • structured the story • developed a meaningful theme
Poetry	How effectively has the poet • used (or not used) rhyme • created stunning word pictures • used figurative language • structured the poem • expressed an otherwise inexpressible idea

USING TEXTUAL EVIDENCE

Prove it! Anytime you write a literary analysis, informational text, or argument, you will be expected to prove your main idea or claim. You draw the **textual evidence** for that proof from the collection of details you have mined during your close readings.

During your close readings, you gathered evidence by taking notes from the work itself. These notes may have included descriptive passages, lines of dialogue, narrative details, facts, examples, statistics, and other kinds of details. In drafting an analysis of a text or in piecing together an informational or argumentative text from several sources, include the evidence in a way that will convince readers of your main idea or claim.

Strengthen your arguments by using relevant quotations from your text or texts that support a point. Work them smoothly into your writing and punctuate them correctly. The following guidelines show how to work textual evidence into a written analysis. They use examples from a literary analysis on a short story by Marjorie Kinnan Rawlings called "A Mother in Mannville."

Guidelines for Using Direct Quotations in a Literary Analysis

1. Always enclose direct quotations in quotation marks.
2. Follow the examples below when writing quotations in different positions in the sentence. Notice that quotations in the middle or end of a sentence are not ordinarily capitalized.

Begins Sentence	"He wore overalls and a torn shirt," observes the narrator (323).
Interrupts Sentence	In his "grave gray-blue eyes," the narrator sees a rare and precious quality (325).
Ends Sentence	The narrator feels that Jerry's integrity makes him "more than brave (325)."

3. Use ellipses—a series of three dots (. . .)—to show that words have been left out of a quotation.
   "For a moment, finding that he had a mother shocked me . . . and I did not know why it disturbed me" (327).
4. If the quotation is four lines or longer, set it off by itself without quotation marks. Indent one inch on the left and leave space above and below it.

   > And after my first fury at her—we did not speak of her again—his having a mother, any sort at all, not far away, in Mannville, relieved me of the ache I had had about him. . . . He was not lonely. It was none of my concern. (328)

5. After each quotation cite the page number of the text in parentheses. The citation usually precedes punctuation marks such as periods, commas, colons, and semicolons. For plays or long poems, also give main divisions, such as the act and scene of the play or the part of the poem, plus line numbers.

Following are examples of using textual evidence in a different kind of writing—an informational research report on the lost city of Atlantis. The sources are indicated in parentheses and would be keyed to a works-cited page at the end of the report.

Examples of Using Textual Evidence in an Informational Report

1. Use a quotation to finish a sentence you have started.

   Example Photographs taken in 1977 of underwater stones are believed to "bear the mark of human handiwork" (Whitney).

2. Quote a whole sentence. If you omit words from a sentence, indicate the omission with an ellipsis, a series of three dots (. . .).

   Example "He suggests that the structures match the description in Plato's Dialogue Critias . . . and that the high mountains of Atlantis are actually those of the Sierra Morena and the Sierra Nevada" (Shermer).

3. Quote four or more lines from a source. For a quotation of this length, skip two lines and set the quotation as a block indented one inch on the left. You do not need quotation marks for such an extended quotation.

   Example Here is how Plato describes the downfall of Atlantis in the dialogue called *Timaeus:*

   > Some time later excessively violent earthquakes and floods occurred, and after the onset of an unbearable day and a night, your entire warrior force sank below the earth all at once, and the Isle of Atlantis likewise sank below the sea and disappeared. (1232)

4. Quote just a few words.

   Example According to Plato, in an "unbearable day and a night" Atlantis was destroyed (*Timaeus* 1232).

5. Paraphrase information from a source.

   Example "Although many have dismissed Atlantis as a myth, some 50,000 volumes have been written to describe and locate it." [Original]

   Curiosity about Atlantis and efforts to locate it gave rise to some 50,000 books on the topic ("Greek Backs Plato Theory"). [paraphrase]

For informational and argumentative texts, including research reports, be sure to verify factual evidence in your sources for accuracy.

Verifying Factual Evidence

- Locate at least two sources that contain the same basic facts.
- Skim each source for specific details, such as dates, locations, and statistics.
- If the specific details in both sources agree, you can probably rely on their accuracy.
- Watch for discrepancies in broader concepts, such as in the sequence of events or in the relationship between cause and effect.
- If you discover discrepancies, use a third source to determine which source is likely to be more accurate.

COMPARING TEXTS

Another way to achieve a deep understanding of a text is to compare it to another text. You can compare and contrast literary texts in many ways. You could, for example, do a close reading of two (or more) texts using any of the same focus points outlined on pages 145–149, and then compare and contrast the way each text addresses that focus point. Following are just a few of many examples.

Two or More Texts of This Type	Focus Points to Compare and Contrast
Short stories	Structure (use of chronological order or flashbacks), theme, plot, character development, point of view, setting, style
Poems	Role of persona, figurative language, rhyme and meter, theme
Biographies	Details of life that are emphasized or omitted in each version; overall sense of person's character and motivation
Informational Texts	Structure, point of view, importance of main idea, support for main idea, language and style, author's purpose, accuracy of information, possible bias
Argumentative Texts	Structure, point of view, significance of main claim, quality of supporting details for claims, logical reasoning, accuracy of information, possible bias, language and style, conclusions

The following chart shows additional ways to compare and contrast texts to deepen your understanding of them.

Types of Texts to Compare	Questions for Comparing Texts
Texts in different forms or genres (such as stories and poems, historical novels and fantasy stories, short stories and novels)	• How is the approach to theme and topic similar in both forms? • How is the approach to theme and topic different in the two forms or genres? • How does their form or genre make these texts unique?
Fictional portrayal of a time, place, or character and a historical account of the same period	• How do authors of fiction use or alter history?
Modern work of fiction versus traditional sources	• In what ways does the modern work draw on themes, patterns of events, or character types from myths, traditional stories, or religious works? • How is the modern work turned into something new and fresh?

continued

Types of Texts to Compare *(cont.)*	Questions for Comparing Texts *(cont.)*
Texts from the same era that approach themes differently	• What was the purpose of each text? • What was the writer's frame of reference or worldview? • Whom was the writer addressing ?
Texts from different eras	• What does each text reveal about social attitudes during the time in which it was written?
Different texts by the same author	• What themes appear repeatedly in works by this author? • What changes in style and/or theme, if any, are apparent in later works by the author compared to earlier works?

Comparing Texts in Different Mediums "Texts" do not necessarily need to be written pieces. In fact, comparing texts in different mediums—such as print, audio, and video—can lead to valuable insights.

The following chart shows some questions to ask when comparing and contrasting texts in different mediums.

Reading a Story, Drama, or Poem	Listening to or Viewing an Audio, Video, or Live Version of the Text
• When you read the text, what do you see in your mind's eye? How do you picture the visual images, the characters, and the setting? • What do you hear—what do the characters' voices sound like? • What are the sounds in the setting? • What can you experience reading a text that you cannot experience when viewing or listening to an audio, video, or live version of the text?	• When you listen to an audio version of the text, what do you experience in comparison to when you read it? Are any elements more vivid? less vivid? • When you view a video version of the text, what do you experience in comparison to when you read it? • What can a video provide that a written text cannot? • How does the experience of a live performance differ from reading a text? • What can a live performance offer that reading a text cannot? • How faithful to the original text is the audio, video, or live version? If it differs in significant ways, why do you think the directors and actors made the choices they did to change it?

You know the techniques writers use to make an impression and impact. They include provocative language, narration that can get inside of characters' heads, and plenty of room for the readers' imaginations to fill in visual and auditory details. Understanding the "tools of the trade" of different mediums can help you make clear comparisons and contrasts.

Techniques of Audio	Techniques of Video	Techniques of Stage
• Actual voices and other sounds in the setting • Possibility of music to help create mood • Room for imagination to fill in visual aspects	• Representation of all sounds and visuals; little left to the imagination • Lighting, sound recording, camera angles, color, focus, and special effects all shape the visual message • Use of background music to help create mood • Editing techniques that place one scene next to another to make a comment	• Representation of some sounds and visuals within the limited scope of the stage • Stage directions that tell characters how to interact in each scene • Lighting and other special effects • Live actors creating a sense of immediacy • Use of music

Sometimes you may be asked to **compare a single scene in two different mediums.** For example, a chilling scene in the book *To Kill a Mockingbird* centers on the shooting of a mad dog by mild-mannered lawyer Atticus Finch. If you read that scene carefully in the book and then compared and contrasted it to the same scene in the movie version of the book, you could evaluate what is emphasized or absent in each treatment of the scene.

Sometimes you may be asked to **compare multiple versions of a story, drama, or poem in different mediums.** How does the stage version of *To Kill a Mockingbird* differ from both the print and movie versions? How do the film and stage versions offer different interpretations of the original text?

AUTHOR BIOGRAPHIES

ISAAC ASIMOV It's hard to think of a writer more prolific than Isaac Asimov. In his 72 years, he wrote or edited more than 500 books. Though he is best known for his science-fiction novels, he wrote on other subjects as well; his writings are classified in every library subject area except philosophy. Born in Russia in 1920, Asimov and his family immigrated to the United States when he was three years old. They opened a candy store, where young Asimov worked and read the science-fiction magazines that were for sale. He began writing at the age of eleven, and by the time he was eighteen, he had sold his first story. As an adult, Asimov earned a Ph.D. in chemistry from Columbia University, then worked as a chemist at Boston University until writing took his full attention. He also served as president of the American Humanist Society from 1985 until his death in 1992. His science-fiction novels, many of which explain difficult concepts in simple ways, are among the most popular books ever written in that genre. Along with Robert Heinlein and Arthur C. Clarke, Asimov is considered one of the three "masters" of science-fiction writing.

DAVE BARRY Born in New York in 1947, David Barry notes in his online bio that he "has been steadily growing older ever since without ever actually reaching maturity." A natural comedian, Barry's writing career began with short humor pieces that he wrote for his high school newspaper. Today his newspaper column is published in over 500 newspapers nationwide. Barry has written 23 books and won numerous awards, including the Pulitzer Prize for commentary in 1988. His nonliterary endeavors have included his involvement in the CBS sitcom "Dave's World," based on two of his books; and playing lead guitar in the rock band Rock Bottom Remainders, made up entirely of authors—including Stephen King and Amy Tan. Barry lives with his wife and two children in Miami, Florida.

RAY BRADBURY Describing the act of writing as "a fever—something I must do," Ray Bradbury acknowledges that he always has "some new fever developing, some new love to follow and bring to life." As if to back up that claim, he wrote his first story at age eleven, on butcher paper. Since then, Bradbury has published more than 500 short stories, novels, plays, screenplays, television scripts, and poems. Many, such as *The Martian Chronicles*, *The Illustrated Man*, *Fahrenheit 451*, and *Something Wicked This Way Comes*, have been best sellers. All have been wildly creative, blending contemporary issues with fantastical science fiction to make observations about the way we live today. Among his many awards are the O. Henry Memorial Award, the Benjamin Franklin Award, the World Fantasy Award for lifetime achievement, and the Grand Master Award from the Science Fiction Writers of America. He received the National Book Foundation Medal for his distinguished contribution to American Letters.

RICHARD BRAUTIGAN Almost immediately after moving to San Francisco in 1955, at the age of twenty, Richard Brautigan became famous as part of the beat movement in poetry and performance. His work first appeared in *Four New Poets* in

1957. In the same year *The Return of Rivers*, a poem of two pages, appeared. Only fifteen copies of this book were published. He frequently performed his work around the country. Brautigan also wrote several pieces of poetic fiction. He traveled about giving readings and lectures until 1972, when he moved to Pine Creek, Montana, and spent several years in seclusion. He continued to write, but in 1984 friends became concerned about an extended period of silence. They broke into his home to discover that he had died of a bullet wound. Authorities concluded that Brautigan had killed himself. Though Brautigan's work has never received a great deal of critical attention, it remains popular with readers. It has been translated into twenty languages and has enjoyed immense popularity in Japan.

Frederic Brown Born in Cincinnati, Ohio, Frederic Brown lived in the Midwest until the late 1940s, when he moved to Taos, New Mexico. After stints as an office worker and a proofreader, Brown became a writer of crime fiction and mystery novels, publishing stories in pulp-fiction magazines such as *Weird Tales* and *Detective Tales*. His first full-length mystery won an Edgar Award. Brown later switched to science fiction to escape crime fiction's heavy emphasis on realism. He was successful in this, too; his work has been inducted in the Science Fiction Hall of Fame. Brown died in1972, yet his work is still gaining the respect and attention of literary critics.

Helen Chasin As an undergraduate student at Harvard, Helen Chasin studied poetry with poet Robert Lowell. In 1967, she was published as a Yale Younger Poet. Her work became well-known and Chasin began working as a poetry workshop teacher herself. As such, she maintained her relationship with Lowell and other accomplished poets while also supporting emerging poets. She taught her students to avoid sentimentality and abstractions in favor of strong, concrete images.

Mildred Clingerman She did not write many stories, but those that Mildred Clingerman did write were so memorable that they won her the lasting loyalty and admiration of many science-fiction fans. The most famous of her books, *A Cupful of Space*, was published in 1961 and is still widely available today.

Carol Farley At home in Ludington, Michigan, Carol Farley has been writing science fiction and fantasy for more than 40 years. She enjoys creating difficult characters and unusual situations because "when every character is wonderful and loves everyone else, and they all live lives of joy and happiness—there can be no story." Farley not only writes, she also leads workshops for young writers to encourage them to think and write expressively.

Nicholas Stuart Gray Born in Scotland in 1922, the family life of Nicholas Stuart Gray was difficult. Gray made up stories even as a child, but his first career was in the theatre, where he worked as an actor, director, and stage manager as well as playwright. His first play was performed when he was only fifteen, and Gray often starred in his own plays. A pioneer in children's theatre, he also wrote several books and short stories, many of which are still available today. Gray died in 1981.

W. HILTON-YOUNG is an obscure writer whose short story, "The Choice," was first published in 1952 in *Punch*, Britain's eminent magazine of humor and satire.

PAUL JENNINGS An Australian writer, Paul Jennings has won many awards, including an Order of Australia for his contributions to children's literature. His short stories and novels are prized for their quirky humor and their keen sense of what it is like to be a child. Jennings was born in England in 1943 but moved with his family to Australia in 1949. He worked as a teacher, a speech pathologist, and an adult educator before deciding to write full-time. In addition to writing stories and books, Jennings tours, tells stories, and gives talks about writing. He also has undertaken scriptwriting for both television and film.

URSULA K. LE GUIN When it comes to writing, Ursula K. Le Guin can do almost anything. She has published six books of poetry, several books of children's fiction, twenty novels, and more than a hundred short stories. She has also published books of essays and translations of the work of other authors. Her work has repeatedly won awards such as the National Book Award, the Pushcart Prize, the Hugo Award, and the Nebula Award, among others. Le Guin's most popular books are those in the Earthsea Trilogy, which have been translated into sixteen languages. Though she was born and grew up in Berkeley, California, Le Guin has lived in Portland, Oregon, since 1958. She protects her private life but occasionally offers writing workshops.

FRITZ LIEBER Born in Chicago in 1910, Fritz Lieber grew up among Shakespearean actors. After serving for a time in the Episcopal Church, he became an actor in his father's company. Lieber moved to Hollywood in the 1930s and acted in a few films, but soon became a writer whose influences included author J.P. Lovecraft, mythologist Robert Graves, and psychologist Carl Jung. He split much of his adult life moving back and forth between Chicago and Los Angeles. Early in his writing career, Lieber also took other jobs, working as a speech instructor, an inspector in a plant making WWII aircraft, and an editor at *Science Digest*. He poured all these experiences into his work, and Lieber's stories won several Hugo, Nebula, and other awards. After his first wife died in 1969, Lieber sank into a three-year struggle with alcoholism. He emerged to write additional prizewinning examples of fantasy and science fiction. Lieber died in 1992.

MARGARITA MARINOVA Bulgarian-born Margarita Marinova has long been interested in life on other planets. In high school, she chaired the Toronto chapter of the International Mars Society and was a three-time winner of NASA's space settlement design contest. Now a graduate student in geological and planetary sciences at the California Institute of Technology, she is working on a project to establish life on Mars. She hopes to be one of the first people on Mars someday.

CHRISTOPHER P. MCKAY A planetary scientist who explores the possibility of life on other planets, Christopher P. McKay earned a Ph.D. in astro-geophysics from the

University of Colorado in 1982. He then went to work at NASA's Ames Research Center, where he remains today. As a scientist at the center, he studies microorganisms in Antarctica, the atmosphere of Titan (one of Saturn's moons), and the geological history of Mars. All this work is aimed at finding clues that will lead to the discovery of extraterrestrial life. Dr. McKay has been involved in actively planning missions and possible human settlements on Mars.

John Frederick Nims Born in Muskegon, Michigan, in 1913, John Frederick Nims was educated at schools throughout the Midwest. By the time he earned his Ph.D. at the University of Chicago in 1945, he was already a respected poet and critic. In addition to teaching at Harvard, the University of Florence, the University of Toronto, the Bread Loaf School of English, Williams College, and the University of Missouri, Nims served as the editor of *Poetry* magazine from 1978 to 1984. Nims authored seven books of playful and witty poetry as well as several translations and various works of criticism. He won awards and fellowships throughout his career. He died in 1999.

Julie Nobles is the Early Childhood Coordinator at the University of Missouri-Kansas City Institute for Human Development.

Robert Priest A Toronto-based poet, playwright, songwriter, and novelist, Robert Priest has published several children's books and fourteen books of poetry for adults. He also has released a number of spoken word recordings and musical performances with his band, the Great Big Face. Priest, whose work has won international attention and acclaim, acknowledges influences from Bob Dylan, Allen Ginsberg, John Lennon, and Prince. His widely anthologized work has been translated into Chinese, French, and Spanish. He is currently at work on a screenplay.

Craig Raine Born in England in 1944, Craig Raine studied at Oxford before taking up a career as an editor and a writer of literary criticism. He published his first book of poems in 1978 to high acclaim, and soon became known for his startling similes. In 1981, Raine became the poetry editor at London's Faber & Faber. Ten years later, he became a fellow of New College, Oxford. The award-winning Raine is also the founder and editor of the literary magazine *Areté*.

Norman Spinrad Born and raised in New York, Norman Spinrad earned a degree from City College of New York. In 1961, he moved to California. He published his first short story in 1963 and his first novel in 1966, after which he embarked on a career as a full-time writer. Spinrad's work has been translated into eight languages, and his 1972 novel *Iron Dream* won the Prix Apollo in France, where Spinrad currently makes his home. Many of his novels and short stories have gone out of print, but some of these have recently found a new publisher—Toxic Press in the United Kingdom. Spinrad has also written teleplays and is currently at work on a screenplay of his 2005 novel entitled *Mexica*.

ACKNOWLEDGMENTS

Text Credits CONTINUED FROM PAGE 2 "Puppet Show" by Fred Brown." Copyright © 1963 by HMH Publications, copyright renewed 1991 by the Estate of Fred Brown. Originally appeared in *Playboy* magazine; reprinted by permission of the author's estate and its agents, Scott Meredith Literary Agency, LP.

"SQ" by Ursula K. Le Guin. Copyright © 1978 by Ursula K. Le Guin; first appeared in *Cassandra Rising*; from *The Compass Rose*; reprinted by permission of the author and the author's agents, the Virginia Kidd Agency, Inc.

"The Star Beast" by Nicholas Stuart Gray. Reprinted by permission of Faber and Faber, Ltd.

"The Water Traders' Dream": Copyright © 1981 by Robert Priest. Previously published as a Dreadnaught Broadside, 1981; in *The Ruby Hat* (Aya Press, 1987); and in *A Terrible Case of Stars* (Puffin, 1994).

"What's Alien You?" by Dave Barry. Reprinted by permission of the author.

Photo and Art Credits Cover and Title Page: Gayle Denington-Anderson, *Hot Summer Night*. Watercolor and acrylic, 22 x 30 inches. Page 3: Georges Méliès, from the film *A Trip to the Moon* (1902) Paris. Bibliothèque Du Film (BIFI), Collection Cinemathèque Française. Page 5: Alfred Worden, *Crescent Earth Over the Lunar Highland*, Apollo 15, 1971, Private Collection. Page 11: Hans Neleman. Page 12: © ColinGray/Photonica. Page21: Otmar Thormann/ Photonica. Page 22: Superstock. Pages 28-29: © John Still/Photonica. Pages 30-31: David Cunningham. Page 32: NASA, Jet Propulsion Laboratory. Pages 36 and 37: Peter Blume, *Winter*, 1964. Oil on canvas, 48 x 60 inches. A.C.A. Galleries, New York. Page 39: Bruce Jensen. Page 45 © Stuperstock. Page 46: Mark Purdom/Photonica. Page 56: Leeanne Schmidt/ Graphistock. Page 61: © 1997 Francisco Villaflor/Photonica. Page 63: National Archives Record Group 341, Project Blue Book Case No. 9318. Page 65: National Archives Record Group 341, Project Blue Book Case No. 9654. Page 66: National Archives Record Group 341, Project Blue Book Case No. 7027. Page 67: National Archives Record Group 341, Project Blue Book Case No. 8398. All from *The UFO Phenomenon*

© 1987 Time-Life Books, Inc. Page 69: Stu Suchit, *Songs in the Key of Life*. Page 72: Jeff Brouws, *Route 60, Arizona*, courtesy Robert Mann Gallery. Page 83: Joseph Cornell, *Americana: Natural Philosophy (What Makes the Weather)*. Smithsonian American Art Museum, gift of Robert Lehrman in honor of Lynda Roscoe Hartigan, © 1995. The Joseph and Robert Cornell Memorial Foundation. Page 84: Francis Bacon, *Study for Nude Figures*, © 1950. Oil on canvas, 77 1/4 x 53 1/4 inches. Courtesy Tony Shafrazi Gallery. © 2000 Estate of Francis Bacon / Artists Rights Society (ARS) New York. Page 91: Francis Bacon, *Study for a Crouching Nude*, 1952. The Detroit Institute of Arts, gift of Dr. Wilheim R. Valentíner. © 2000 Estate of Francis Bacon / Artists Rights Society (ARS) New York. Page 92: © Bettmann/Corbis Page 93: TL, © Bettmann/Corbis; TR,
© Hulton-Deutsch Collection/Corbis; ML, © Bettmann/Corbis; MR, Chatto and Windus; BL, © Bettmann/Corbis; BR, Secker and Warburg. Page 94: TL, Putnam; TR, Jay Kay Klein; M, Bettmann/ Corbis; BL, Gnome Press (Merril Collection). Page 95: TL, Penguin/Corbis-Bettmann; TR, Corbis/ Bettmann-UPI; Gollancz (Bruce Pennington); ML, Liaison Agency; MR, Ballantine Books; BL, Ace Books; BR, © Bettmann/Corbis. Page 96: © Stephen Webster/Photonica. Pages 101 and 103: © Wataru Yanagida/Photonica. Pages 104-105: © Hiroshi Hara/Photonica. Page 105: Superstock. Page 106: © T. Shimada/Photonica. Pages 121 and 133: Martin Jarrie. Pages 122 and 132: Ferruccio Sardella. Page 134: John Sims, *Willow Tree*; Somerset levels, England.

Every reasonable effort has been made to properly acknowledge ownership of all material used. Any omissions or mistakes are not intentional and, if brought to the publisher's attention, will be corrected in future editions.